BUCKET

~ TO ~

GREECE

Volume 2

V.D. BUCKET

Editor: James Scraper
Cover: German Creative
Print Format: The Book Khaleesi

Other Books in the
Bucket to Greece Series

Bucket to Greece Volume 1:
A Comical Living Abroad Adventure

Chapter 1

Lost to the Shredder

After a morning spent grappling with the complexities of the three Greek genders my brain was reduced to mush. Whilst it was perfectly logical that the declinable article preceding the name of my good friend Spiros was masculine, I struggled to get to grips with the concept of random things such as bunches of spinach, bicycles and egg cups, having assigned sexes. It was all terribly confusing. It had just been drilled into me during class that linguistically a sheep was male, but what if

I happened across a ewe in my stroll through the village? Should I address it as male or female?

I couldn't even pick Marigold's brain since she'd skipped our weekly Greek lesson in favour of her monthly get together with the Greek ladies of the village to beautify the cemetery. These meetings appeared to involve rather more coffee drinking and gossip than actual weeding, but provided a great opportunity for my wife to develop new friendships in the community of Meli. The mountain village of Meli had been our new home since upping-sticks from Manchester to a new life in the sun almost three months ago, and we were keen to integrate into village life.

Carrying my pile of completely indecipherable Greek textbooks into my new home office I was shocked to catch my brother-in-law Barry engaged in an act of wanton destruction. Rushing forward I attempted to stop him from feverishly feeding the first forty pages of my painstakingly penned 'moving abroad' manuscript into the shredder.

"I have to do it Victor, it's for your own good," a sheepish looking Barry said.

"Are you crazy?" I shouted.

"Marigold made me do it," Barry confessed. "Anyway she may have a point, do you really suppose anyone will be riveted by your account of Marigold's difficulties in locating a foreign lavatory that is more than a hole in the floor, or in long-winded descriptions of hygiene violations you detected on the ferry over to Patras?"

"You're the one who advised me to make it authentic and pad it out with lots of details of local colour and customs," I remonstrated, seizing hold of the wad of paper in a desperate attempt to prevent it from being chewed to ribbons. The shredder gobbled its way through the pages, rendering my efforts futile, quite amazing considering it was the only electrical appliance we'd brought over from England that still seemed to be working on the Greek two-pronged circuit.

"I'm sorry Victor, but I promised Marigold I'd get rid of it, she complained you portrayed her in a most unflattering light," Barry apologised.

"But the whole point of me dragging out the old Bucket name as a pseudonym is so that no one can identify us if the book becomes a runaway best seller," I argued. "Marigold would retain her anonymity."

"Perhaps you should switch your nom de plume to Burke now it transpires that the woman who abandoned you in a bucket as a baby turns out to be a person named Violet Burke," Barry suggested. "If she ever turns up here she's got a lot to answer for, saddling you with the unfortunate initials of V.D., with their disease riddled connotations. It's a good job you were adopted and name changed quickly; there's not much to choose between being a Bucket or a Burke. I suppose you could add the whole sorry saga to the book though, it would make an engrossing storyline."

"I cannot believe you think that the heartless woman who abandoned me in a bucket should be used as cheap fodder for mass entertainment," I protested.

"Probably best to wait and see if she actually turns up as she threatened," Barry conceded. "It could be a bit difficult to pad out her character since you've never actually met her."

Ignoring Barry's flippant lack of tact I fingered the ripped shreds of paper, lamenting, "But all those wasted hours agonising over the perfect words to put on the page, now lost forever."

"Well it's not as if you have to give up on the idea of writing a book, just start again fresh and make it read less like a critical report you've penned for the Foods Standard Agency. Marigold says you still haven't got the hang of using exclamation marks instead of full stops, but if you keep at it you might pick up the style."

Marigold's obsession with moving abroad books had left her with the misguided impression that the pages ought to be indiscriminately littered with superfluous exclamation marks. I'd be as likely to take literary advice from my wife as I would from the cat. I decided I would start over, but keep the manuscript well hidden from my wife's prying eyes and the cats' destructive claws.

"How did Marigold persuade you to do her dirty work for her?" I asked, reflecting that perhaps the book would be improved it I made it more Greek centric and dispensed with the intimate details of my leaving do, marking the close of my illustrious career as a public health inspector. Perhaps including the speech I gave was a tad unnecessary. I decided to take a pragmatic approach; I would re-write the book and at least the pile of shredded paper would serve as much needed mulch for the compost heap.

"She threatened that if I didn't destroy it she'd show Cynthia the photographs of me with that haircut," Barry confessed.

"Not the mullet," I cried, wide-eyed with horror that my wife would resort to such devious blackmail tactics to get her brother do her bidding.

"She played really dirty, she threatened to show the mullet one with the moustache," Barry winced. It wasn't a pleasant recollection. Even though he had insisted at the time that it was the height of fashion, the tacky mullet and moustache combined to make him look a real plonker.

"I can see why you gave in to her blackmail. It's a bit early in your relationship for Cynthia to be confronted with the most embarrassing images of your past when you're still trying to make a good impression."

"It's good of you to be so understanding," Barry said in relief. It was impossible to fall out with my brother-in-law, even if he had just shredded my literary masterpiece.

Barry had flown over from England, ostensibly to visit us, but in reality using us as an excuse to spend time with Cynthia, an English woman living in Meli whom he'd met when he'd first driven us and our worldly goods over to Greece in one of his removal vans. It was obvious that the pair of them were head-over-heels. Since Marigold was keen to encourage the budding romance in the hopes Barry would spend more time in Greece, it struck me as unlikely that she would follow through with her threat to flash an unbecoming picture of her moustached and mulleted brother in front of Cynthia. I decided to ask Marigold where she'd stashed the offending photo; it would amuse me to introduce it as a conversation starter with some of the elderly Greek widows in the village who had taken rather a shine to Barry. It would no doubt prove helpful in expanding my Greek vocabulary to include the synonyms of frightful.

I intended to spend the afternoon stuffing my brain with as many Greek food related words as I could cram in, in preparation for the evening ahead. Earlier that morning Marigold had popped into the village shop for some *kourabiedes,* almond biscuits. She thought a crafty decorative sprinkling of icing sugar may be enough to fool the ladies at the cemetery gathering into thinking they were homemade delicacies hot from her own oven. She returned from the shop with the dreadful news that Dina, one half of the couple that run the local taverna, had suffered the misfortune of falling off a haphazardly balanced olive tree ladder, breaking her arm in the process.

"Not just any old arm either, but the one she favours when cooking," Marigold relayed. "Poor Nikos is at his wits end and is talking of having to close the taverna until she's got her arm back. He just can't manage alone and his useless son Kostis is off on one of his hunting trips, chasing down wild boar."

"Well it makes a change from chasing women. That's terrible about Dina, is she in much pain?" I asked in genuine concern. Dina was a delightful lady; she always had a warm smile on her face despite her heavy workload helping Nikos in the fields and the taverna. It was a lot of work for a couple in their late seventies.

"Nikos said she's muddling along. The hospital plastered her up and sent her home, but she can't cope with her usual kitchen duties. Nikos said at any other time of the year he'd likely manage, but now the nights are getting colder it's his busiest time of year. The wood burner is a big draw, people can get warn without burning their way through their own log piles."

"What bad luck that he must close and lose

business," I commiserated, thinking I would sorely miss the opportunity to pop in if he closed.

"I knew you'd think that Victor, which is why I volunteered your services to help out in the kitchen. You start this evening," Marigold announced.

"You volunteered me without even consulting me first," I said, mortified she had taken such a liberty. "Really Marigold, I'm not sure my Greek culinary skills are so finely tuned I can feed a room full of people."

"Nikos cooks the meat on the outdoor grill Victor, as you well know; all you'll need to do is throw a few salads together and fry the chips," Marigold said impatiently.

"It won't be easy living up to Dina's chips, they are without doubt the best I have ever tasted," Barry said, his face adopting a dreamy look.

"I told Nikos you'd pop in late afternoon before he opens because Dina can't manage to peel the potatoes without her arm. If she's up to it she'll sit quietly by in the kitchen to give you a few pointers this evening," Marigold said.

"That's sure to be helpful as I can barely understand a word she says," I pointed out, my sarcasm lost on Marigold. "You are patently aware that Dina's taverna duties stretch to far more than simply tossing a few salads together; she also serves the food from the kitchen at the tables."

"Yes, but it's not as though you'll need to take orders Victor, it's not exactly fine dining with a choice of menu," Marigold snapped, reminding me that the staple taverna menu was bread, cheese, salad and whatever Nikos grilled, with fried potatoes. "Anyway, it will be the perfect opportunity for you to practice your Greek. Since the customers won't be able to get away from you when you try to talk to them, you'll have a captive audience. Plus you said you wanted something to occupy you now you've retired, that would bring in a bit of pocket money."

"Look on the bright side, "Barry piped up. "You'll probably be on the same hourly rate as Guzim. I'll bring Cynthia along for dinner, shall I? It should be a hoot to see you in action."

Chapter 2

Burnt Sunshine

Marigold had really gone and landed me in it this time. The prospect of being responsible for preparing traditional Greek food and serving it to a taverna full of critical Greek locals certainly presented a challenge. When I'd mentioned I may fancy a little job in the future to occupy me on a part-time basis, I'd been thinking more along the lines of acting as a tour guide for British tourists holidaying in the area. I had an interesting stack of historical tomes on the Mani which I intended to read my way through so I could present myself as a fountain of local knowledge.

New to early-retirement, I was still enjoying the change of pace, my days no longer ruled by the list of restaurant and takeaway kitchens I'd been duty bound to inspect in my glittering career as a public health inspector. Thus far my new life in Greece had not seen me descend into idleness: my first month had been occupied with overseeing the work of Vangelis, a local builder, in modernising the old village house we'd purchased from the local undertaker, Spiros, who had inherited it from his dead uncle. The overgrown garden presented an enormous challenge, but with the help of Guzim, the Albanian who lived in the stone shed at the bottom of the garden, the overgrowth was being restored to order and the first vegetable seeds planted. Once the initial frenzy of activity associated with moving had abated we began weekly Greek lessons, and I started to pen the now shredded book about our experiences moving countries. Not ready for the scrap heap quite yet, I fully intended to keep busy.

My former career exposed me to some of the most disgustingly foul restaurant practices, inspecting insanitary and infestation riddled establishments, the owners clearly deleterious in their duties of abiding by strict hygiene regulations. Naturally this left me suspicious of eating in restaurants where the kitchens remained unvetted by my experienced eye. The local taverna I was about to help out in featured a soot stained ceiling festooned with dusty mosquito clogged cobwebs. It had initially struck me as a filthy dump that would fail a health inspection miserably, yet the food that emerged from Nikos' outside grill and Dina's archaic kitchen was the best I had ever tasted, everything being home grown or reared for the grill. I soon realised that the filth was superficial, being limited mainly to the dining area. Dina may be a lovely woman with high standards of personal hygiene yet she takes a very lax attitude to mopping and dusting, but she does keep a clean enough kitchen, if not exactly scrupulously.

Nevertheless I reflected that if I was to help out in the taverna it would have to be thoroughly scrubbed. I couldn't in all conscience compromise on my exacting standards and serve food prepared in anything less than the most hygienic conditions. Realising a monumental task awaited, as soon as lunch with Marigold and Barry was finished I raided my stock of rubber gloves, scourers, bleach and sanitiser to take along to the taverna.

"Victor, Nikos isn't expecting you to start work until early evening," Marigold said.

"I cannot in all conscience work in that place until it has been thoroughly scrubbed." I replied. "Perhaps you'd like to come along and help since it was you that landed me in it."

"You have to be joking. I've done quite enough for today and plan to spend the afternoon curled up with a good book. I was up at the crack of dawn baking *kourabiedes* to take along to the beautifying the cemetery gathering, and then spent all morning pulling weeds out of graves," Marigold stated, sending me one of her withering looks when I choked with laughter at her delusion she had actually baked the shop-bought biscuits.

There was no sign of Nikos when I arrived at the taverna, but the door was ajar. Surmising he was busy in the fields I took stock of my surroundings, realising I had an insurmountable task before me in licking it into cleanliness. I began by clearing all the detritus of the previous evening's dining into bin bags and generally tidying up. Neither Nikos nor Dina seemed bothered that old newspapers littered the place or that discarded plastic packaging from bottled water was piled randomly in dusty corners. Holding a mildewed copy of *To Vima* at arm's length I was not completely surprised to discover it was more than three years out of date, the headlines dating back to June 1999.

The next item on my agenda was tackling Dina's kitchen. Tutting with disapproval I carried the vat of olive oil she used to fry her famous chips in outdoors, careful to throw it on the nearest patch of grass. Disposing of oil down the sink would likely cause a blockage and I was clueless if the sewage truck that pumped the waste from the local sceptic tanks would be able to cope with a fatberg. It struck me that Dina probably hadn't changed the oil in the grimy and greasy fryer since the turn of the century.

Next, I treated the kitchen to a vigorous scrubbing followed by a deep sanitising. Moving into the dining area I swept up the detritus and then considered removing the cobwebs hanging from the ceiling; since the mosquito season had finished they served no useful purpose. Despite being six feet tall I was unable to reach the ceiling even when I balanced on a chair. Not willing to be defeated I took out my mobile phone and called Vangelis the builder to see if he could pop round and lend me a ladder.

Fortunately since Vangelis was working locally, he was round in a jiffy with the requested ladder. During the course of the work he had done on our house Vangelis had proved to be a good friend and we always enjoyed running into one another. We often shared an evening together at the taverna, but now he was justifiably curious as to why I was up his borrowed ladder brushing the cobwebs from Nikos' ceiling. I explained the predicament Marigold had landed me in and Vangelis agreed that the old place could definitely benefit from a good sluicing down.

"The Athena no longer bothers to shower and dress up to come here to eat. She shower when she get home, she say the place make her to feel the grubby," Vangelis told me.

I shared his wife's sentiments; it was always a case of dressing down when we ate at the taverna, preferably in something that was due for a wash since the stench of fried chips clung to whatever we wore. Marigold bemoaned the missed opportunity to dress up for dinner but the local taverna suited me. I could enjoy a glass or two of Nikos' spectacular *spitiko* wine without worrying about driving home. I was the designated driver in our marriage since Marigold refused to learn to drive the left-hand drive Punto.

"You know Victor, even with all the scrubbing that ceiling will never come the clean, it is too blackened from the much soot from the *somba*," Vangelis pointed out.

"It would certainly benefit from a fresh coat of paint," I concurred. "I suppose Nikos just doesn't have the time, he's in the fields all day and grilling all night."

"He is too the busy to notice. What say you we give it a fresh coat now, I have the spare paint in the van," Vangelis suggested.

By early evening the taverna practically gleamed with cleanliness and boasted a freshly painted orange ceiling. I wasn't too sure of the colour but Vangelis had a job lot going spare.

"Anyway it is not the orange, see, it say on the tin it is burnt sunshine," Vangelis said as we stared at the ceiling.

"Well it's definitely an improvement on soot stained," I said, wondering if it had ever been white to begin with.

"Give the greeting to the Marigold. The Athena was very impressed with the *kourabiedes* she brought along this morning. She say from now on she will bring the shop bought too, rather than getting up before the dawn to do the baking," Vangelis said with a knowing wink.

With Vangelis gone I decided to go home, shower, and catch forty winks before returning to manage the kitchen that evening. About to leave, I suddenly remembered that I still had to peel my way through an enormous potato mountain in preparation for that evening's chips.

Chapter 3

Guzim Gets a New Shirt

I was just stepping out of the taverna to head home for a shower and change of clothes before returning for my first evening shift as a volunteered chef, when Spiros cycled by. He was still defiantly helmetless in spite of the rakish scar he bore from being flung over the handlebars when his bicycle had an unfortunate encounter with a pot hole. It appeared my frequent lectures on optimum health and safety guidelines for cyclists obviously went in one ear and out the other.

"Victor, it is good to see you my friend. What are you doing coming out of the Nikos' place at this early hour, he not start the grill until nine?"

After explaining my situation as a volunteered chef, having promoted myself from kitchen skivvy, Spiros commented he expected the taverna would be very busy when word got round the village that a foreigner was working the kitchen.

"I have the good news for you Victor. I have persuaded Papas Andreas to bless your house *methavrio*," Spiros declared.

"Would that be *methavrio* in the literal sense of the day after tomorrow, or in the more general sense of some extremely random time in the future?" I enquired.

"Ah Victor, I see you are growing the Greek sense of the humour," Spiros laughed. "The Papas will be there the morning of the day after the tomorrow. Be sure to have the things ready for him, he will to bring the holy water and the basil, but you must to provide the candle and the small gift for his trouble."

"It's very good of him considering we aren't regular church goers, not being orthodox," I said.

"I arrange it Victor, the Papas know he owe you the favour after all."

I struggled to think why on earth the Papas should be under the impression he owed me a favour. I had seen him hurrying around the village, distinctive in his orthodox black vestment and stove pipe hat, but always in the distance, and never to speak to. I had heard he was apparently a very busy man, stretching himself rather thin by overseeing churches in three different villages.

"He is the son of your neighbour, the Kyria Maria. He is very gratified you find the way to put the stop to the mother's disgusting habit of burning the plastic daily," Spiros explained. "Her habit made him feel much the embarrassment."

"It was a great relief to scheme up a way to stop her nasty plastic burning habit," I said. For the first month in our new home we had been plagued with toxic smoke wafting over from Maria's daily bonfire, a habit she had acquired during a two-decade feud with Spiros' uncle, her neighbour before us who had plummeted to his death from the roof. She had finally promised to put an end to the practice when I wheedled an invitation for her to a pool party thrown by Harold, a particular obnoxious ex-pat.

Harold liked to befriend any local British or any random tourists he would trawl for in the nearest beach bars, hoping to wow them with his superior pool. He sorely regretted his move to Greece, but couldn't sell the traditional house he had ripped all the traditional features from. He had the deluded idea that Greece had tried to invade England during the war and he kept his distance from the locals, clueless they considered him an entitled boor. He had seemingly made it his life's mission to befriend me and drag me over to admire his pool.

"Kyria Maria bore the ear off anyone who will listen about how she went to the pool party at the foreigns. She is the only non-British person in the village to have been in the pool," Spiros said.

"Harold's deluded sense of superiority has alienated most of the British," I said, delighted he had taken to snubbing me. Since Maria spoke not a word of English, and Harold and his wife Joan not a word of Greek, it had amused me greatly to watch them attempt to get the old woman out of their pool. From what I could gather they had taken to avoiding answering their door just in case it was Maria demanding repeat access to their precious pool.

"Yes, soon he will be the desperate enough to start wanting the, how Harold say, the Greek peasants as friends, now all you British avoid him," Spiros chuckled.

Bidding goodbye to Spiros I continued home, stepping into the garden before heading upstairs. I immediately spotted Guzim, the Albanian who lived in the stone shed at the bottom of the garden, helping himself to oranges from my trees. A tall fence had been erected around the stone shed to safeguard the privacy of all parties and a hole knocked in the garden wall to provide Guzim his own access without traipsing through my garden; nevertheless Guzim still wandered into the garden at will, having quite obviously worked one of the wooden planks in the fence loose with this very purpose in mind.

Guzim hurried over for a chat as soon as he caught sight of me, even though our level of conversing resulted in constant miscommunications. Still at least Guzim's misunderstanding that I was a mentally defective homosexual had been cleared up satisfactorily. My increasing vocabulary allowed me to throw the odd word out in the wrong tense and gesticulations proved quite effective.

Guzim offered me one of my oranges, the fresh aroma of citrus tempting me to peel it immediately. As I savoured in the luxury of eating fruit plucked from my own orange tree, Guzim decided to get up to his old tricks by pulling at my purse strings through my heart strings. Pulling on his shirt sleeve to show off a ragged rip, he bemoaned "*den einai kalo,*" which I translated as meaning "no good." He then spewed out a string of indecipherable Greek. I recognised random words in his monologue but failed to piece together 'money', 'bus', 'shirt', and 'wife' into any semblance of a coherent sentence. I presumed he was telling me he couldn't afford a new shirt to replace the ripped one since his wife in Albania ate all his money, but I failed to see where the bus came into it.

Vangelis had given me clear warning that Guzim would try and manipulate me into giving him things, using the excuse he was permanently poor since he sent all his wages to his wife in Albania. Vangelis warned me Guzim would try to take advantage of what he would perceive as a gullible rich foreigner and not to fall for his sob stories since he earned the going rate for his labours and drank all his wages. On this occasion the tears coursing down Guzim's face as he ranted on about his ripped shirt did move me, even though I recognised I was being suckered. The regular work I'd given him in the garden which supplemented his earnings from labouring had dried up with the onset of winter. I felt a tad guilty that by reducing the days I hired him to just one day a week I had exacerbated his pitiful poverty.

Gesticulating for Guzim to wait for me in the garden I went into the house to see if there was a suitable shirt in my wardrobe that I wouldn't miss too much. My attention was drawn to a long sleeved tee-shirt emblazoned with the slogan 'Be Clean and Hygienic' that Barry had gifted me one Christmas as a joke, now lying in a rumpled heap on the wardrobe floor. Although I appreciated Barry's attempt at cheap humour I would never be caught dead in a tee-shirt, being strictly a button down kind of guy. I couldn't imagine how it had ended up in my Greek wardrobe since I'd had a good clear out when packing. Reaching down to remove the tee-shirt I noticed it was serving as a make-shift bed for Clawsome's new kittens, the devil-spawn of Cynthia's ugly mutant rapist Tom. Shooing the kittens out of the wardrobe I gave the tee-shirt a brisk shake. I certainly wouldn't miss it and Guzim was always so shabbily attired I presumed he'd be grateful for anything, even if it was covered in cat hairs.

Guzim received the shirt with exaggerated gratitude, throwing himself to the ground and grasping my knees, no doubt convinced such an effusive display would persuade me to part with my belongings on a more regular basis.

Chapter 4

Marital Chat

"Victor, have you been upsetting the new kittens again?" Marigold accused.

"They may be feeling a tad upset if they overheard me saying it was time we found them good homes," I retorted.

"How can you be so cold-hearted? We can't possibly separate Clawsome from her babies," Marigold scolded.

"But they could go and live with their father," I pointed out. "Let Cynthia's vile raping

Tom take responsibility for its mutant off-spring."

"I have no intention of creating a scene with Cynthia by throwing out baseless accusations. We can't be certain her cat was responsible for Clawsome's pregnancy," Marigold said, wilfully blind to the visible evidence that the kittens had popped out looking more like rabbits than cats, branded with Kouneli's distinctive black stripe on their mutant faces.

"We don't want to say anything that will upset the apple cart or cause tension between her and Barry. She's practically family after all?" Marigold continued.

"How so? Don't tell me Barry has already gone and proposed, they've only been walking out for five minutes."

"Well we'd only been walking out for three months when you proposed Victor."

"That was different; we had to hurry things along with Benjamin on the way," I said tactlessly, hurriedly adding, "But of course I would have married you anyway."

I decided it would be best to keep my own counsel about giving my unwanted shirt to Guzim. Marigold hadn't really taken to the Albanian in the shed since discovering he'd been playing me for a fool by gifting me the fruit from our own trees. Nor did she like the way he kept popping up in our garden unexpectedly by manipulating his scrawny frame through the loose plank he'd deliberately fashioned in the new fence.

I remembered to share the news that Papas Andreas would be calling in to bless the house and that we would need to present him with a small gift when he'd finished waving his basil sprig.

"I've no idea what sort of thing to give to a Papas as a gift," Marigold said, her face contorted by disquiet as she tried to think of something suitable. "We haven't even met him so I've no idea what would go down well."

"I will leave it to you to decide," I said.

"I've seen him scurrying about the village; it's hard to miss him with that unruly grey beard. Perhaps we should buy him a nice electric razor," Marigold suggested. "He'd look much younger if he shaved it off."

"Marigold, the beard is a requirement for orthodox clergy," I said, exasperated that she had obviously paid no attention when I'd read her the passage from my book on orthodox traditions.

"Well perhaps a beard trimmer then, to tidy it up. I'm told it's quite an honour to have the house blessed. Who do you think we should invite to the ceremony?" Marigold asked.

"Spiros naturally, we wouldn't have this house to be blessed if not for our good fortune in meeting him. And Vangelis, of course. We really ought to include Kyria Maria from next door," I said.

"Oh Victor, I'd rather not, I can't abide the way she pokes her fingers in any bottled condiment that she finds a novelty."

"Then I suggest you hide the condiments before her arrival as it may offend Papas Andreas if we exclude his mother."

"I do hope he hasn't inherited her propensity for sticky fingers," Marigold sighed before exclaiming, "What on earth will I feed them? It's such short notice."

"There's no need to get in a panic about it, I would think a selection of cakes and biscuits would be appropriate for the occasion. Vangelis commented that your shop bought biscuits apparently went down very well this morning."

"Drat, how could they possibly tell they were shop bought, I'll never live it down? I must start baking now. Actually I'll start in the morning, I'm joining Barry and Cynthia for dinner at the taverna; they insisted on inviting me along, saying it wasn't right I must eat alone when you'll be off having fun."

"You wouldn't be eating alone if you hadn't volunteered me to work in the evenings," I pointed out, flouncing off to my stint as chef in the local taverna. Fun indeed.

Chapter 5

Chef Delusions

A couple of elderly Greek gents had already claimed the seats closest to the smoky *somba*, or wood burner, huddling over its heat when I arrived for my shift at the taverna. I was glad to step into the warmth; there was more than a hint of a nip outside. Nikos greeted me by announcing I was cutting it fine, he was ready to fire up the grill, obviously saving his more hearty greetings for paying customers. He failed to mention how spotless the place was or how the fresh coat of paint was a huge improvement on the soot-blackened ceiling. Dina greeted me with much more warmth than her husband, almost dealing me a fatal blow when she threw her arms around me in gratitude for coming to the rescue, forgetting the plaster cast encasing her broken arm could double up as a deadly weapon.

"Dina sit in the kitchen to give to you the advice," Nikos said.

"That's most kind," I said, hoping she wouldn't get under my feet and cramp my culinary style. "Whilst I do consider myself quite skilled as a chef of modest talents, preparing Greek dishes is all still a bit new to me."

"Chef," Nikos spluttered, doubling over in laughter. Ignoring his slight I strode into the kitchen ready to spring into action.

"I leave you to it; you cope with the woman's work?" Nikos asked in a mocking tone, blatant scepticism written all over his handsome face.

"I'm sure I will manage," I replied, confident in spite of my nerves. I would be far more at home inspecting the kitchen for hygiene violations rather than cooking in it, but at least if such a thing as a Greek health inspector should turn up unannounced I was satisfied the place wouldn't be closed down for a gross breach of regulations.

"There seem to be something different about the place, but I not to put my finger on it," Nikos said, staring around the taverna quizzically, completely oblivious the whole place had been thoroughly deep cleaned and treated to a new coat of paint on the ceiling. "Ah, that is it," he suddenly exclaimed, the puzzle clearly solved. "Someone has been in for the copy of *To Vima*, we Greeks like to keep up with the news."

I didn't bother to respond or confess I had slung the mildewed old newspaper out without considering one of the villagers had been waiting their turn to read it. The notion that the news headlines from 1999 could still count as news in 2002 was asinine in my opinion.

Dina pulled on my sleeve to attract my attention, nodding towards the two elderly gents still waiting to be served. Grabbing a basket I filled it with bread and carried it over to their table. Dina was obviously not impressed with my service, hoisting herself up from her seat to demonstrate that the bread should have been placed on top of the *somba* to slowly toast. It had completely skipped my mind that the change in season had introduced this variation to the menu. The effort of moving clearly took its toll on Dina who was obviously in pain despite her best attempts to hide it. Guiding her back to her chair I indicated by gesture that she should leave it to me, and then busied myself preparing the salads and oiling the cheese. Dina pulled on my sleeve again to mime the act of drinking; I rushed back to the table to pour homemade wine from a plastic bottle into tall water glasses.

The villagers began to arrive at a pace steady enough for me to just about cope. I had just served salad and cheese to Spiros, who had joined Marigold's table, when I noticed a young man enter the taverna: I use the term young in the relative sense since anyone under seventy stood out as young in this village of pensioners. The new arrival was wearing the exact same shirt I had given to Guzim earlier. There was no question it could be a coincidence, there was no possible way the identical shirt could put in a sudden appearance in a remote Greek village. I considered perhaps the man now wearing my shirt had broken into Guzim's stone shed to steal it, but decided to tackle the subject diplomatically before calling the police.

As I approached his table with a basket of bread he dismissed it with a curt wave, grunting

"*Mono beera*," meaning only beer. His strong guttural accent identified him as a fellow countryman of Guzim and I pondered perhaps I had been hasty in presuming he was a shirt thief when the more likely explanation was that he'd borrowed it from his friend. There was no time to broach the matter since Dina needed me back in the kitchen to start frying the potatoes to serve alongside the goat Nikos was grilling.

Having emptied the oil from the fryer and scoured it thoroughly during the afternoon, I now needed to put my hands on some fresh oil for frying. Dina raised her hands to her head in bewilderment when she noticed the now gleaming fryer was bereft of oil. Clucking her tongue in disapproval she exited through the side door to fetch Nikos to translate.

"Where is the fry oil?" he shouted, staring at the now oil free fryer in consternation.

"I gave it a thorough boil-out following the latest advice on deep-fryer cleaning standards; the oil was well overdue for a change, it certainly looked a bit past its best," I said. Staring at me as though I'd lost my marbles Nikos shrugged in disbelief, asking, "But what you think give to Dina's potatoes the taste she is famous for?"

Realising there was nothing else for it he indicated I should pass him a new sixteen kilo tin of olive oil to pour in the fryer. Tutting impatiently when I struggled to haul the heavy tin from the floor, he took over, lifting the tin and pouring the contents into the fryer as though it weighed no more than a feather. As the oil was poured Dina kept up a steady stream of indecipherable Greek to which Nikos shrugged his shoulders, saying "*ti boro na kana*?" meaning 'what can I do?' It appeared my well-meaning gesture of scouring the grungy fryer was anything but appreciated and they would have preferred it if I'd left the fryer in its original greasy state.

With the potatoes in the fryer I started to prepare more red onions, aware the latest arrivals were waiting impatiently for their salad. Slicing the onions released the chemical irritant syn-propanethial-S-oxide, causing tears to freely roll down my face. Dina addressed me, saying "*yiati klais*." Having no clue that she was asking me why I was crying, I simply shrugged Greek style, prompting Dina to head outside again to drag her husband in to translate.

"Victor, I am the sorry I was the angry about the oil, now Dina is the angry at me for making you to cry," Nikos apologised, before adding, "But it is not the manly to cry over such the small matter of lost oil ."

"I am not crying, my tears are an involuntary reaction to slicing the onions," I snapped, wondering how long Nikos could remain dry eyed whilst tackling potent onions. Nikos turned to Dina in frustration, waving an onion under her nose to clarify the misunderstanding. Looking at me sheepishly she shrugged, but I was touched by her genuine concern that I may have been reduced to tears by Nikos' brusque manner.

My fried potatoes were not nearly as well received by the customers as the ones made famous by Dina, apparently lacking that special something that aged oil infused with grime, old food particles and the memory of potatoes past, provides. Unable to conceal his disappointment that the potatoes weren't up to Dina's usual standards Barry nevertheless took pity on me, lying to my face when he said, "These chips aren't half bad Victor."

"And the salad is so fresh," Cynthia joined in.

"The bread have just the right golden crisp from the *somba*," Spiros complimented.

"You're going to smell like a chip shop later," Marigold complained.

Running the kitchen single-handedly was extremely hard work, especially as the heat from the *somba* was intensified by the heat from the deep fat fryer. I was in such a rush to prepare and serve the food that I hardly had a second to practice my Greek on the captive customers. It appeared to amuse the regular locals that I was working in the taverna, but they nodded appreciatively when I presented them with their food, even if it wasn't quite up to the usual standard. I received a few hearty back slaps for stepping into the breach left my Dina's missing arm. I noticed Marigold deep in conversation with a grey haired English couple I hadn't yet met but knew lived nearby; there was only time for the briefest introduction to Milton and Edna when I served them their chips.

Fortunately I was able to grab a breath when Nikos served the goat; I took the opportunity to approach the Albanian wearing my shirt, still glugging the same bottle of Amstel he'd been nursing all evening. It would be a bit of an exaggeration to describe the exchange that ensued as an actual conversation, more a list of the most basic Greek words flung about between us.

I began by pointing at his shirt and saying in Greek, "shirt me," to which he responded "no shirt me." We repeated this exchange several times in pantomime style before I recalled the Greek word for gift and spiced up the exchange by managing, "shirt me gift Guzim," to which he replied "shirt me pay Guzim."

Overhearing this pathetic exchange Cynthia kindly intervened to ask the Albanian wearing my shirt how much he had paid Guzim for it, to which he replied "five euros." By this point Barry had recognised the shirt he'd gifted me for Christmas. Appearing offended that I was obviously unappreciative of his present, he demanded to know what was wrong with it and why I had sold it.

"Really Barry, your choice of clothes leaves a lot to be desired, have you ever seen me wearing anything so casual? Have you ever seen me wearing anything with a slogan? You know I'm a smart shirt and tie man all the way," I blustered; dismayed he had caught me out disposing of his gift.

"It's all the fashion Victor and I thought you'd like the reference to your hygiene obsession."

"I am no more obsessed with hygiene that you are an arbiter of fashion Barry, as I think your attachment to that mullet proved. Anyway I didn't sell it; I took pity on Guzim and gave it to him because his was ripped, not expecting he would attempt to make a quick buck off the shirt off his back."

"That will be for the bus fare," Spiros interrupted. "He not got enough the money to get the bus back to see the wife in Albania."

"I expect he drank the bus fare," I snapped, my sympathy for Guzim wearing thin. I presumed a few extra shifts in my garden would help him to come up with the money to visit his wife at Christmas.

The Albanian wearing my shirt started muttering under his breath. Cynthia kindly translated, telling me, "He says you ripped him off, charging so many euros for a shirt covered in cat hairs."

"Tell him his reasoning is quite ridiculous, I didn't rip him off, it was Guzim who sold him my shirt, if I'd have sold it to him I would have charged extra for the cat hairs," I shouted, exasperated by the ridiculousness of the situation.

Cynthia spoke to him some more in Greek, before telling me, "He is very angry and wants to sue you under the trade description act. He had no idea the slogan on the shirt reads 'Be Clean and Hygienic' and takes it as a personal insult; he says he had a bath only last week. Guzim told him the slogan read 'Albanian and Proud.'"

The Albanian drained his beer and stormed out of the taverna angrily when Cynthia translated that I had no intention of giving him a refund.

"Fire," Spiros cried, his eyes riveted on sudden flames flaring up outside. Spiros' cries alerted Nikos who came running to grab the fire extinguisher, pushing me out of the way and practically sprinting by me. Rushing outside he unleashed the white foam over the fire that had been carelessly started when the Albanian threw a lit match into the greenery after lighting a cigarette. It was hard to believe one negligently discarded match could create such a sudden inferno. Nikos stomped back inside muttering that some idiot must have poured petrol on the grass for it to have combusted so quickly. It suddenly occurred to me that the area of the fire coincided with the exact spot I had disposed of the old cooking oil. I decided it might be prudent not to mention this salient fact. If Nikos asked I would claim I had poured the old oil down the sink and let him sweat, imagining a great big fatberg could block his pipes at any moment.

The Albanian wearing my shirt staggered back inside, white with shock from his near combustion, the hem of my shirt sleeve visibly burned beneath its coating of foam. Without bothering to ask I served him another beer.

"Eat Victor," Nikos commanded, calling me away from the pile of washing-up I was elbow deep in and placing a plate of grilled goat in front of me. I sank wearily into a chair, glad of the humble yet tasty fare. "You come again to-morrow, yes? I could not to manage without you, and the customer not to complain."

I was bone-tired after a full afternoon of cleaning and peeling potatoes, and an evening of skivvying in the kitchen and rushing between tables. I looked at the elderly couple, Dina clearly in pain from her broken arm and Nikos so proud that he hated to ask for help. "You can count on me until Dina has her arm back," I said.

"Good," Nikos replied. "Now to wages."

"There's no need for that, I'm happy to help

out in the circumstances," I told him.

"Victor, you to insult me, I pay the honest wage for the honest work. We say three euro the hour, I know it is too much the generous but you try the hard. But no more to pour the oil in the grass," he said with a wink, revealing he had known all along I was responsible for the fire. Filling my glass to the brim with excellent *spitiko* wine he once again stared quizzically around the empty taverna, saying, "There's something different but I not to put my finger on it."

He remained oblivious that a decade's worth of filth had been expunged from the ceiling and every surface. Finally after another five minutes of perplexed staring he pounded his fist on the table. Pointing towards the ceiling he shouted, "How in the world did that to happen, the ceiling before was white, how it come to be the orange?"

"I think you'll find it's actually burnt sunshine," I teased, creased with laughter that he'd never apparently noticed the once white ceiling had been black for years.

Chapter 6

This Make the Victor Popular

Bone-weary from my work in the taverna I strolled home, the full moon rendering the light from my torch unnecessary, though it still amused me to shine the beam and watch the stray cats scurrying from whatever doorway they'd bedded down in for the night. It was close to midnight and the night was cold but the air crisply fresh, just a tang of olive wood smoke discernible from the villagers' wood burners and open fires.

Marigold was waiting up for me with a mug

of cocoa, eager to tell me Barry was definitely smitten with Cynthia. She announced we would be calling on Milton and Edna the next morning for elevenses, assuring me they were an interesting couple I would get along with. We hadn't met them before since Milton hadn't got out much whilst recovering from his hip replacement.

"Of course it means I'll have to start baking at the crack of dawn to have everything ready for the house blessing ceremony on Wednesday morning," Marigold sighed. "I was rather hoping you could whip up one of your lemon drizzle cakes Victor, they always go down a treat."

"I will certainly try and fit it in between social calls and another long shift in the taverna," I said sarcastically.

"Don't exaggerate Victor, it's only the evening shift, the whole day is your own," Marigold said, seemingly unaware I'd been toiling nonstop since lunchtime. "Anyway I'm dead on my feet, do make sure you leave your clothes on the balcony before coming to bed, you smell like a chip shop."

Showering in freezing water I cursed Barry for his too frequent showers and remembered I needed to get Eduardo the electrician round to connect the water tank to the electric. With winter approaching the solar panel produced less hot water, most of which Barry had apparently used up by showering excessively to make a good impression on Cynthia. By the time I'd changed into my pyjamas Marigold was snoring softly, ear-plugs bunged firmly in place to prevent my snoring from disturbing her. I reflected that skivvying in the very basic local taverna was a bit of a come down from my illustrious career as a health inspector, but it had nevertheless felt worthy in its way to step into the breach occasioned by Dina's broken arm. I laughed at the thought of my generous rate of three euros an hour; back in Manchester that would be considered exploitation as the minimum wage was over four pounds an hour.

Drifting into sleep I was disturbed from my slumber by a raucous din emanating from the bottom of the garden. The sound of raised voices punctuated by shouts was soon replaced by the noise of a drunken scuffle. Climbing out of bed I peered through the window, spotting the figures of Guzim and the Albanian wearing my shirt, clearly illuminated in the moonlight and now engaged in an all-out brawl, in my garden no less.

"Really, you'd think they'd keep it to Guzim's side of the fence," I said to myself, opening the window and hollering for them to keep the noise down. Guzim, distracted by my voice, was slow to avoid a thump in the face from the shirt wearer. "I expect he'll have a real shiner tomorrow," I muttered, satisfied to see they were at least now moving their skirmish to Guzim's side of the fence. Climbing back into bed, careful not to disturb Marigold who needless to say had slept soundly through their noisy carousing, I made a mental note to memorise the necessary Greek words to give Guzim a piece of my mind the next time I saw him.

In spite of the late night I was up at my usual crack of dawn the next day. I always appreciated the early morning peace, savouring my first shot of caffeine whilst watching the sunrise. Stepping onto the balcony I took a moment to enjoy the stunning view, the white crests of waves in the distance hinting the sea was choppy today and the mist hovering over the mountains suggestive of a downpour. I knew I was being used when Catastrophe brushed herself against my leg with fake affection, manipulating me into filling the bowls with cat food. Though I would never admit it to Marigold I had grown quite fond of the imported cats; less so of the mutant kittens that were always getting under my feet.

Mindful of Marigold's request that I bake one of my scrumptious lemon drizzle cakes I set about rubbing and whisking the ingredients, thinking this cake should be my best ever since it would be created with lemons plucked from our very own trees. Wandering into the garden to pick the fruit I noticed with annoyance that a broken chair leg had been chucked in the garden through the loose plank in the fence. Although mildly concerned that the shirt wearing Albanian may have used Guzim's solitary chair as a weapon against him, I was still too annoyed by their rowdy late night shenanigans to check if Guzim was still in one piece. I dismissed him with the cursory thought, 'let him stew in his hangover.'

Back in the kitchen I treated myself to another coffee. Inspired by the citrusy tang of the tree-fresh lemons I'd collected I decided to make an extra lemon drizzle cake to take along to the taverna that evening. I was hopeful a tempting slice of after dinner cake offered to the customers may take the sting off the chips not being quite up to par. Nikos may even decide my cake was so delicious he would add it to the non-existent menu, leading me to establish a side-line as a baker of renowned patisserie goods. Deciding that a smidgen of the local Greek spoon sweets on the side would complement the cake to perfection, I strolled over to the village shop to purchase some of the bitter lemon rinds in syrup, thinking I must find the recipe and make my own next time.

I was quite surprised by the unusually warm reception I received in the village shop, prompted by one of the village men who'd eaten in the taverna the previous evening rushing over to shake my hand, announcing to the shop at large *"einai o xenos sef."* His statement was easily translatable to me as 'it is the foreign chef' even though it hadn't cropped up in my archaic phrasebook, since the Greek word for chef was almost identical to the English version. His words encouraged other villagers I hadn't yet had the pleasure of being introduced to, to come over and shake my hand.

I recognised one man who approached me as being a very near neighbour. He could often be seen sitting on a hard backed chair on his doorstep engrossed in a book. I thought perhaps he was a kindred spirit since like me he always made an effort to dress smartly, never venturing across the threshold of his door without a tie. Speaking in very slow and deliberate English he introduced himself: "*Yassas* chef, I am Dimitris, tonight I eat your food in the taverna. You do the good thing to help Nikos. Please excuse my English, I learn from the book. Perhaps you can correct when I speak incorrect to improve my English."

"Your English is much better than my Greek," I said, tentatively adding in Greek that I was taking Greek lessons but finding the classes very difficult.

"Victor, you just tell me you are learning Greek in the taxi. You must put the stress at the beginning of the word to say class. See, we can correct each the other."

"Correct each other," I corrected him.

"I think the taverna will be very stuff of people tonight. They hear of the foreign chef and come to eat," Dimitris said. I bid him good morning, telling him I looked forward to seeing him in the taverna that evening and practicing our respective languages together.

Marigold was busy in the kitchen by the time

I returned, half-a-dozen brand new Greek cookery books lying on the counter, their pages open to reveal a tempting assortment of cake recipes.

"I don't think I'm quite up to tackling anything really tricky like *baklava* or *bougatsa* just yet, you know how my pastry leaves a lot to be desired," Marigold said. I decided it would be diplomatic not to confirm her pastry was always a lumpy mess, with an inevitably rock-hard crust and soggy base.

"I thought I'd stick to the basics and opt for cakes that aren't so different to English ones," Marigold continued. "I'm going to bake, now let me see if I can try and pronounce them, a *karidopita* walnut cake, a *ravani* coconut sponge, a *portokalopita* orange cake, and a *kormos* chocolate log. I'll need some Tia Maria for the log thingy."

"An excellent selection my dear, they'll be spoiled for choice. I did a lemon drizzle cake earlier."

"Oh Victor, that's marvellous, you must have made an early start, I presumed you were having a lie-in."

Marigold's words would have astounded me if we hadn't been married for thirty-five years. Not being a morning person it was perfectly feasible she could get up without even noticing I was not still in the bed beside her; which I rarely was.

"I was up with the lark, quite surprising considering the late hour I got home and the disturbed night I had thanks to Guzim and his fellow countryman engaging in a drunken brawl in the garden," I said.

"I must have slept through it. I hope it didn't disturb Barry, he needs his beauty sleep to look his best for Cynthia," Marigold said. "You'll have to have words with him Victor."

"I'd rather not get involved in the budding romance between Barry and Cynthia," I said.

"Don't be so obtuse, I didn't mean have words with Barry. You must have a word with Guzim, we can't have common brawls going on in the garden; people may get the wrong idea and think we are having a domestic."

Just then Barry and Vangelis made an appearance, Barry eying the lemon drizzle cake hungrily.

"Hands off, that's for the house blessing ceremony tomorrow," I snapped, before modestly announcing, "It appears my evening shift in the taverna has made me quite popular. The place should be packed tonight with people eager to sample the food of the foreign chef."

In reality I was actually quite worried that I would be able to juggle the food preparation and serving at tables if the place was indeed packed.

"You're hardly cheffing, Victor. It's only salad and chips," Marigold bluntly pointed out.

"I think you may have got the wrong end of the stick Victor," Barry chimed in. "From what Cynthia said, being able to understand what the Greeks were saying, they'll be turning up to see the Brit who Nikos has managed to get skivvying for just three euros an hour, they think it's a hoot. I think you've deluded yourself into thinking your role of kitchen assistant has turned you into a chef."

Barry's words immediately burst my bubble, leaving me deflated.

"No Barry, the Cynthia make the mistake, her Greek not so perfect," Vangelis contradicted. "The people want to see the foreign who do the good turn and step in to help the Nikos because the Dina has only the one arm. This to make the Victor popular, that he rally round in the hour of need."

Vangelis' words immediately re-inflated my ego, assuring me my gesture of volunteering to help Nikos out during this time of Dina's incapacity was appreciated as an act of solidarity.

"It was me who volunteered him," Marigold piped up, determined to take the credit. "Now, what can we do for you Vangelis?"

"I came to look the loose plank in the Guzim fence. Victor tell me it upset you Marigold when the Guzim sneak through the hole into the garden."

"Can you manage to fix it without Victor? I hadn't realised the time, we're due round at Milton and Edna's for elevenses," Marigold said.

"I think when it comes to fixing the defect it is better without the Victor," Vangelis confirmed.

"Well bang as loud as you like," I encouraged. "I want Guzim to feel every thump of your hammer piercing his hangover."

Chapter 7

The Sorry Saga of the Destitute Orphans

Milton and Edna were thrilled to welcome us for elevenses since they didn't receive many visitors or get out much. Edna whisked Marigold inside to dry off by the fire since a sudden torrential downpour had drenched us on the walk over, whilst Milton corralled me in the doorway, asking if I'd mind terribly carrying a few logs inside from the wood pile since he found it tricky to manage with his stick.

"We budget for one meal out a month, got to keep the old date night going, and what a delight it was to run into your wife last night," Milton told me as I hauled wet wood. "It was a bit of a shock old chap to find a Brit waiting on tables at the local hostelry."

"I prefer to think of myself as European," I said.

"Well quite," Milton said, a tad flummoxed by my comment. "Don't get me wrong, I'd be up for it myself as a way to boost the old income if it wasn't for my dodgy hip."

Carrying the wood through into the living room where every spare seat was claimed by a dozing cat, Milton told me to chuck one of the logs onto the fire.

"Are you sure dear?" Edna questioned worriedly. "It isn't time for the next one yet."

"I think we can afford a bit of extravagance since we have visitors old girl, we can always go up to bed an hour earlier to make up for a spot of reckless burning," Milton protested breezily.

Edna's reluctance to add another log to the fire made me wonder if the couple were obsessively frugal or if they were down on their luck. I began to suspect the latter when Edna spooned only one teaspoon of instant into the coffee pot for the four of us. There was no offer of biscuits or cake, making me wish I'd brought along one of my lemon drizzles. I immediately invited them to attend our house blessing ceremony the next morning since Marigold was planning to bake enough cakes to feed the five thousand.

Their home could best be described as chic shabby, but much more shabby than chic. There was a definite chill in the air despite the fire, leaving me to wonder if it had just been lit for our benefit and if they usually spent the winter days huddled up under blankets. Catching me looking around Edna apologetically said, "I'm afraid the place is overdue a good bottoming, I got behind with spending all my time at the hospital."

"Edna's been marvellous, she moved into the hospital with me when I had the old hip replacement. She was wonderful, sleeping in a chair next to my bed," Milton proclaimed.

"Oh, what devotion," Marigold gushed, apparently oblivious to my suspicion that Edna had stayed by her husband's bedside as they probably couldn't afford the expense of hiring a private nurse.

"I felt guilty putting the cats out to fend for

themselves, but Milton has to come first," Edna said.

"It was a bit tricky in the hospital since we haven't mastered the old Greek lingo yet," Milton said, surprising me as I thought they had lived out here for several years and ought to be fluent by now. "I was a tad concerned in case I woke up from the op to discover they'd replaced the wrong hip, but I have to say they were marvellous, quite marvellous."

"And the relatives of the other patients couldn't have been nicer, always trying to have a chat even though we couldn't understand a word they said. There was one lady who brought me food from home every day so I wouldn't have to rely on the hospital canteen, such kindness," Edna said.

The conversation inevitably turned to what brought us to Greece and to how we were settling in. In turn Marigold asked how long they had been in Meli and what made them make the move to Greece.

"We came over here in ninety-five because the cost of living in London was getting a bit much on the state pension, in comparison Greece was dirt cheap under the drachma. In hindsight we should have chosen somewhere less expensive than London when we relocated to England from Kenya after I retired."

The news that the couple had lived in Kenya didn't surprise me as they had the air of colonials about them.

"We got this place for a song with the bit of capital we had left after I'd been swindled out of our life savings," Milton admitted quite openly.

"How terrible to be swindled, and how despicable that someone would take advantage of vulnerable pensioners. Couldn't the police do anything?" Marigold asked.

"Afraid not old girl, I hold my hands up though, it was all down to my own stupidity," Milton said.

"Don't be so hard on yourself dear," Edna told him. "It could have happened to anyone."

"Yes, but it happened to me and I still feel guilty that I've stuck you with a penurious old age," Milton said.

"The important thing is we still have each other and if we have to be mired in poverty I'd rather it be here in the sunshine," Edna said, seemingly unaware that it was cold and raining. "So long as the cats don't go hungry, we can suffer anything."

"Indeed, we do love it over here, it's just a

pity we aren't as nimble on our feet these days and can't get out as much as we'd like," Milton said.

Sipping the disgustingly weak coffee we chatted about life in Greece. I remained curious about the swindle Milton had lost his savings to; he didn't strike me as the gullible type. With a little prodding he opened up about his misfortune, saying it was worth the embarrassment of revealing how he'd been conned if it would spare just one other innocent from falling for the same scam.

I listened in fascination as Milton described how he'd been an early convert to the wonders of the internet and email. Having always been the gregarious type he liked to strike up correspondence with strangers in far-flung lands; unfortunately he didn't recognise one correspondent had nefarious intentions to part him from his bank balance, though in Milton's defence not much was known about email scams in the earliest days of the internet.

When a young man made email contact from a refugee camp in Guinea in 1995 Milton was moved by the man's bravery. Barely out of his teens, Kafumba painted a harrowing picture of how he fled from the war raging in Liberia after watching the brutal machete murder of his parents. Kafumba was now responsible for his eleven younger siblings, distraught that they were reduced to living under the intolerable conditions of the camp where food was rationed and water almost unattainable."

Milton paused from telling his tale, allowing me chance to clear my throat, a technique I adopted to cover the snort that had involuntarily escaped me at the thought of a refugee camp where the orphans were deprived of food and water yet supposedly had full access to the internet. Call me a sceptic, but the scammers must have seen Milton coming.

Milton continued the sorry saga, explaining Kafumba's greatest dream was to pay for his siblings' education so they could make a better life for themselves, but his father's fortune was frozen in a Liberian bank account, the authorities refusing to release it until Kafumba could provide the details of a foreign bank account it could be transferred to. Milton was eager to help, thinking it terrible that the twenty million pounds Kafumba's father had amassed as the Liberian Minister of Finance with a side-interest in diamond mines could not be released to provide a better future for Kafumba's orphaned family.

I had always wondered what kind of muppet fell for these obvious scams and now here was Milton, who appeared to be a thoroughly decent chap, sitting before me, a testament to human naivety. Milton admitted that the small percentage of the fortune Kafumba offered him in return for his help in releasing the frozen funds had been tempting; he planned to treat Edna to a round the world cruise with the profits. However this was secondary to his noble aim of ensuring a better life for the destitute orphans. Milton arranged the release of funds with the foreign remittance department of a bank that was later proved to be non-existent, the scammer inevitably cleaning out his bank account.

"I don't think I'm the cruise type anyway," Edna interjected. "I don't blame Milton, he was only thinking of the poor orphans."

"It was stupid of me, I hold my hands up, but back in the early days of the internet no one knew these kinds of scams existed," Milton sighed. "They didn't just fool me. The head of the humanitarian aid charity at the refugee camp must have been taken in too because he verified Kafumba's identity."

I reflected that even after being well and truly scammed, Milton remained a gullible fool, blindly unaware that he had never received a single communication from an actual humanitarian nor from an actual refugee camp.

"Of course nowadays these scams are so popular they even have a name, you should watch out for the advance fee fraud Victor, I'd hate to see you duped too," Milton warned.

I didn't give voice to my rhetorical thought of 'do I look like a complete moron?' leaving Marigold to more politely express it by saying, "Victor is far too much of a stickler for making sure every detail is stamped and fully fact checked; it would be impossible to dupe him."

"Well there's no point crying over spilled milk," Milton said, eyeing the dying embers of the fire before chucking another log on, despite Edna's worried look. At the rate he was going they'd be tucked up in bed long before the evening news. "And now that the old hip has been replaced I'm full of energy and ready to embark on a new career to reverse our fortunes."

"That's admirable," I said, thinking Milton was a real trooper, refusing to let circumstances get him down.

"A new career?" Marigold questioned.

"It's so exciting," Edna trilled. "Milton has started to write a book."

"Not a moving abroad book," Marigold blurted, clearly annoyed at the thought Milton may have stolen her idea of how to keep me occupied by writing about our exploits in moving to Greece.

"Oh no, I've no time for that sort of guff, I'm penning an erotic novel," Milton said with nary a blush.

Chapter 8

In the Swing of Village Life

Marigold could hardly contain her mirth, collapsing into laugher at random moments.

"I just can't get over the thought of the very proper Milton penning porn," she snorted, sieving icing sugar over the *karidopita*.

"Not porn Marigold, erotica, there's a subtle difference," I said. "I wonder if Edna is his muse."

"Oh don't Victor; it's too much to think of that terribly nice pair of twee pensioners getting all hot and steamy under the covers," Marigold chortled.

"It may be the only way they can stay warm," I said, recovering my composure as I reflected it wasn't even winter proper yet and they were already rationing their wood supply. I wondered if there was a discreet way to sneak some additional logs onto their wood pile without them noticing. They struck me as the type who would be mortified by acts of charity unless they were the ones being charitable.

"Still, I'd rather he dabbled in erotica than write a book similar to yours Victor, it could be that Milton has a better handle on the use of exclamation marks and you can do without the competition. Now, do you think we have enough cake for tomorrow?"

Marigold's baking had taken over every surface in the kitchen in preparation for the house blessing ceremony the next morning. There wasn't enough time to drive up to town, where the shops re-opened in the evenings, to buy a gift for the Pappas, without risking being late for my shift at the taverna. I needed to be there early to peel my way through another potato mountain. Instead Marigold sent me back to the village shop to buy him a bottle of whiskey, having been assured by Vangelis that imported scotch was always a hit with the clergy. I was hugely relieved that she'd given up on the notion of presenting him with a beard trimmer; I considered such a gift much too personal and potentially insulting if Papas Andreas interpreted it as us thinking he was a bit lax with his personal grooming.

Returning from the shop I noticed there was no sign of Guzim in the garden even though it was his allotted day of labour.

"He's probably still nursing his hangover," I muttered in annoyance, wandering into the garden to round him up. Vangelis had done a sterling job of patching up the fence, thus I was forced to walk the long way round and clamber through the hole in the wall to reach Guzim's shed. There was no response when I rattled the shed door and no sound of life from within. I hoped that the previous night's kerfuffle hadn't escalated to a murderous degree, resulting in the Albanian wearing my shirt disposing of Guzim's body under the shed. Fortunately I couldn't spot any signs of freshly dug holes in the fifty centimetre perimeter between Guzim's shed and the fence.

"There's no sign of Guzim out there, it's the

first time he's ever let me down," I announced on my return to the house.

"Perhaps he's done a runner," Marigold said hopefully, having never taken to the shed dweller. "At least there'll be no chance of him making off with all the cakes tomorrow, if he has vanished."

"I'd no intention of inviting him anyway," I said. "I consider him selling my shirt and then getting drunk in the shed deplorable behaviour. Still it's not like him to not turn up for his gardening shift."

"There's nothing you can do about it, it's not as though you can report the disappearance of an illegal," Marigold reasoned.

I conceded Marigold had a point but made a mental note to have another rattle on the shed door if Guzum hadn't put in an appearance by the next afternoon.

"Are you off somewhere nice dear?" I asked, suddenly noticing my wife was dressed up to the nines, looking far too glamorous for an evening in the local spit and sawdust taverna.

"I'm off down to the coast with Barry, there's still a few restaurants open out of season apparently. I told him you wouldn't mind if he drives the Punto, after all you can't expect me to stay in every night whilst you're off having fun," Marigold said.

"Just make sure he keeps the windows down in case his travel sickness returns," I advised. The local traditional vinegar and honey remedy had done wonders in curing Barry of his travel sickness woes; he remained clueless the remedy was a fabricated invention.

"To think, all those years, the nausea must just have been in his head," Marigold sighed, amazed by the placebo effectiveness of the dud remedy.

"I'd like to remind you that spending my evening elbow deep in chip fat hardly constitutes fun, thanks to you volunteering me," I said in response to her accusation that I would be off having fun.

"But I know you see it more of a social thing than actual work," Marigold argued.

The taverna was busier than the previous evening, word indeed having spread that a foreigner was playing chef apparently enough to attract a crowd. Dina made a terrible fuss over me, clucking my cheek and ruffling my hair in gratitude that I'd turned up to help out again. Nikos appeared quite sombre. He confided he'd not been expecting so many customers and now he was about to insult them with inferior food.

"Come now Niko, my chips and salad aren't that bad surely," I protested.

"No, is the fine. But today I take Dina to the doctor to look the arm and we have to wait for many hour. I have no the time to prepare the meat. I have the shame to say the souvlaki on the grill is second-class meat from the supermarket," he whispered, embarrassed to be caught out serving something he hadn't reared.

My comment that probably no one would notice didn't go down well, so I revealed the lemon drizzle cake I'd brought along as a sweet treat for the customers.

"Is shop bought?" Nikos asked, staring at it suspiciously.

"No, I baked it myself," I replied.

Nikos flounced off to his grill, muttering something about foreigners coming in with fancy ideas. The sight of the cake made Dina so emotional she burst into tears and rushed out after her husband.

Nikos was duly dragged back inside to translate. It turned out I couldn't even understand a woman's emotions as the cake wasn't the cause of Dina's tears. Nikos explained she was at her wits end wondering how she would bake the bread for the village on Friday morning without her arm. "Everyone expect the bread from Dina, she upset she never miss a Friday, not even the time she gave birth to the Kostis."

Hating to see Dina so upset I confessed I had a little experience with baking bread and would be glad to come along to lend a hand. Dina immediately stopped crying and Nikos smugly said, "Excellent, be here at five Friday morning."

"That's a tad early even for a lark like me," I said.

"There is the much to do," Nikos countered before flouncing back to the outside grill. I suddenly remembered Nikos showing me the outside bread oven where Dina baked the loaves for the village. It had completely slipped my mind until this moment that Dina didn't use modern methods. I began to worry I may have bitten off more than I could chew, suspecting there may be a subtle difference between bunging some packet ingredients into my automatic bread maker and baking bread over twigs.

The arrival of new customers created quite a stir. The middle-aged couple that walked in were so smartly dressed they stuck out like sore thumbs amongst the villagers, the man very dapper in an elegant three-piece-suit and tie, the woman sparkling in a sequin number. Dina rushed forward to greet them, exchanging kisses and showing them to the table closest to the warmth of the somba, turfing the two old men who were already seated there out of their chairs before dusting the seats down with her tea-towel. Then she rushed outside to drag Nikos away from the grill.

Nikos appeared, hurrying to respectfully greet the newcomers as though they were important dignitaries. I speculated the newcomers may perchance have Mafia connections since it was not like Nikos to make such a fuss or act so humbly. There was something familiar about the man, but I couldn't quite put my finger on it; perhaps he was a local celebrity who I'd caught on the local television station.

Nikos rushed into the kitchen, pushing me out of the way. He hastily cut into my lemon drizzle cake, placing two clumsily sliced pieces onto plates that he then presented to the well-dressed celebrities, or Mafia clan; I still hadn't made my mind up on the matter. When Nikos returned I pointed out that the cake was for after dinner, but he brushed me off saying, "This is the important man, you think I give to him the nearly week old bread. Let him eat cake."

"Who is he?" I asked.

"It is the important man, he is the bank manager. I hope your cake is the good enough for him Victor. You promise me it not the shop-bought rubbish."

"I baked it with my own fair hands," I assured him.

"What a night for the important man to honour my humble establishment, the night I grill the inferior shop-bought *souvlaki*," Nikos bewailed.

I knew I'd seen the man before but I hadn't recognised the always dishevelled and casually dressed bank manager who was usually enveloped in a haze of cigarette smoke. I considered it quite bizarre that he should dress down for work and dress up to the nines to come to what has to be the most basic spit and sawdust taverna in the whole of the Mani. Nikos looked at me with new respect when the bank manager spotted me in the kitchen, waving and calling out my name in greeting.

With the previous night's experience under my belt I was able to juggle my respective roles of preparing and serving food more adeptly. The customers humoured me by ignoring my butchered Greek when I tried to converse, careful to speak slowly in Greek for my benefit. Word had apparently spread round the village that I had something to do with the now orange ceiling, resulting in much discussion about the unusual choice of colour. The general consensus was that although the colour was a bit garish it made a nice change from the old white. It seemed Nikos was not alone in failing to notice the ceiling had been soot-blackened for years.

I was delighted to extend a personal welcome to the bookish and tie-wearing Dimitris when he arrived, pleased to accept his invitation to join him for coffee on his doorstep the next afternoon. It would be a wonderful opportunity for us to practice our respective languages on each other. Unfortunately he declined my invitation to the house blessing ceremony, pleading a prior engagement. He struck me as a tad shy, selecting a quiet corner seat, electing to eat on his own rather than joining the general company.

I was very surprised when Marigold and Barry put in an appearance since they were supposedly dining down on the coast. "Harold was holding court in the restaurant we'd chosen," Marigold said with a grimace. Enough said; there was no need for further explanation. Harold was a local ex-pat, a beer guzzling boor who liked nothing more than to boast about his swimming pool to a captive audience. We made a point of assiduously avoiding him and fortunately he had now taken to snubbing us. Still there was no point in Marigold putting herself in a potentially embarrassing situation.

"Thank goodness I made an effort to dress up," Marigold said, spotting the bank manager and waving enthusiastically, absolutely thrilled to accept his invitation to join them; pointing out what a dolt I was for serving them cake before their *souvlaki*.

Dina sat quietly in the kitchen, the pain of her broken arm clearly etched on her tired features. Every now and again she clucked my cheek fondly, telling me in Greek I was such a good boy. I hoped she wasn't getting any ludicrous ideas that I could be her permanent replacement, this was strictly a standing-in temporarily arrangement. Suddenly Dina's tired features were transformed, her face glowing with happiness as she cried "*agori mou, to moro mou*," rushing from her chair to envelop her baby boy Kostis in a smothering maternal hug. I felt a stab of disappointment, presuming Kostis had turned up to help out his mother in the taverna. I may not want the position permanently but I wasn't quite ready to jack in the towel just yet; I was quite enjoying being in the swing of village life.

Nikos abandoned the grill to greet his son. Kostis had not arrived alone; he was accompanied by a pretty young lady of about thirty who he introduced as his new girlfriend Eleni. It struck me that Kostis had not been off hunting wild boar after all. Dina was beside herself to welcome Kostis' girlfriend, gushing effusively over how pretty she was and showering her with kisses. Eleni appeared overwhelmed by the attention, holding onto Kostis' hand shyly.

"Victor, bring the cake," Nikos commanded. Joining me in the kitchen to supervise my slicing he confided, "Nearly forty the Kostis, this the first time he bring home the girl, it mean he must to marry. Look to Dina, she is the radiant, her Kostis marry and soon we to have the grandbabies. Such the girl too, Eleni is the schoolteacher in town, is good for Kostis to have the respectable wife."

"I'm delighted for you all, congratulations,"

I said, adding "I suppose I'm out of a job now Kostis is here to help you run the taverna."

"What the rubbish you talk Victor, Kostis no good to help, you think he make the salad, the potatoes, as good as the foreign chef? Phhh, the truth the Kostis not care to help the mother, he want the freedom before he settle down to village life with the wife. After he marry the Eleni move in with us and help Dina in the taverna, for now you to carry on."

I looked over to Eleni, wondering if she realised her potential in-laws planned to take over her life. There were no schools locally for Eleni to teach in; her future would be mapped out producing babies and taking over Dina's duties in the taverna. It was one thing for a couple used to a life of drudgery, toiling all day in the fields and running a basic taverna in the evenings; it was quite another for a young woman from town to adapt to this life. Kostis had never struck me as half the man his father was, lacking both ambition and a strong work ethic, content to carouse and hunt. Still he had done his duty in Dina's eyes by bringing home a girl he planned to marry; once married he would settle in the village and devote himself to his duty of carrying on the family name. I hoped the look of devoted love so expressively written on Eleni's face would survive a move to the village and the grinding slog of menial work.

Naturally Kostis' arrival with his intended was cause for celebration; Nikos was easily persuaded to play the *bouzouki*. As the customers joined in with a sing-along I noticed Dimitris slipping quietly into the darkness, a torturous look on his face.

Chapter 9

A Traditional Blessing

We were blessed with brilliant sunshine and a pleasant rise in temperature on the morning of the house
blessing, most welcome after the previous day's
rain. I was quite looking forward to the occasion
and the chance to observe some orthodox traditions first hand, appreciative of the honour of
welcoming the priest into our home.

Marigold, for once, was up not long after
the lark, busying herself laying out the food for
the buffet spread. Whenever she had been

invited into a Greek home she had been over-whelmed by the amount of food on offer and was determined to match the Greeks in hospitable offerings. In addition to the lemon drizzle, *karidopita*, *ravani*, *portokalopita* and *kormos* cakes, the sweet selection also included an enormous sherry trifle she'd whipped up. As the ceremony was being conducted mid-morning she decided a selection of sandwiches and sausage rolls would be ideal to accompany the mountain of cake.

"Dina's bread is a bit dense for sandwiches. Victor pop over to the shop for a sliced loaf," Marigold suggested.

"It's a good job Nikos is too busy in his fields to come along, you know how he feels about shop-bought food," I teased.

"Oh, can't he make it, what a shame. Still it saves me from having to pass off these frozen sausage rolls as homemade," Marigold said. "Shop Victor, hop to it, and see if you can pick up some cress while you're there."

Unfortunately it appeared the Greeks didn't do cress so Marigold's egg and cress sandwiches ended up bereft of the cress. The sliced bread felt quite stiff and dry, most likely designed for the toasties the Greeks seemed quite big on; I hoped the guests wouldn't mistake the sandwiches for cardboard offerings. There was plenty of choice though, with tinned salmon and cucumber, or cheese and pickle to choose from. Neither of us was too sure about the wisdom of pairing feta with pickle but Marigold made the good point that the Greeks seemed to eat feta with everything.

"I'm so glad it's stopped raining so we won't need to mop up wet foot prints," Marigold observed as I threw open the windows and the balcony doors. "Now, let's run through the checklist before our guests start to arrive. All the food is spread out for after the blessing, what else do we need Victor? Oh yes, the candle, I suppose that should go in the centre of the table."

"It looks a bit bizarre to have an Easter bunny novelty candle in the middle of your spread," I pointed out.

"You were the one who said my scented ones wouldn't be suitable, the woman in the shop assured me that novelty candles are used for church processions and we will be processing around the house after all," Marigold said. I imagined the woman in the shop had been glad to palm off her old Easter stock and hoped it wouldn't make the priest consider we were taking the occasion frivolously.

"And we've got the scotch as a gift; I wrapped it up so we won't embarrass the priest by publically implying he likes a tipple," Marigold added.

Spiros was the first to arrive and Marigold immediately demanded his opinion if everything looked right for the occasion.

"You forget the icon to go with the candle and the serving bowl for the water to be blessed in and turned into the holy water," Spiros said.

"You never mentioned a bowl or icon before Spiro," I said in exasperation.

"I must have, I am the sure. It is no matter, you must to have the old icon lying around the place, my uncle had the many."

"I know where I can get my hands on one," I said triumphantly, grabbing the gaudy reproduction icon depicting our Lady of the Sign, Platytera, currently used to disguise the fuse box. I propped the icon up in the centre of the spread next to the novelty bunny candle.

"Well I've no idea what we can use for the holy water; the trifle is sitting in my best serving bowl," Marigold wailed. "Do you think we could get away with the washing-up bowl?"

"Please Marigold, not to get so the flap, the wash-up bowl is I think the little disrespect but the soup bowl will to do. This not after all the traditional house blessing, the Papas will make the allowance for your strange foreign ways," Spiros said.

"What do you mean, it isn't a traditional blessing ceremony, you told me it was?" I protested.

"Victor I tell to you the Papas Andreas do the blessing as the favour. I know how much you to like the Greek custom, so I fix for you to feel, how you always say, to fit in. It is traditional for the blessing only to take the place on or after the Feast of Theophany in the January. Today the people will to think you are the very honoured and important to have the ceremony at the wrong time."

Our guests began to arrive and I was pleased to welcome a merge of cultures. The British contingent was represented by Barry and Cynthia, and Milton and Edna. From the Greek side we had Kyria Maria, Dina, Vangelis and Athena, and of course Spiros. Panos of the grapevine fame hadn't appeared and I hoped he was merely held up. Athena announced she couldn't stay long as she'd left Kyria

Kompogiannopoulou under the dryer in her kitchen, mid-perm. Dina, her eyes riveted on the trifle, said she was delighted to have this opportunity to socialise during the morning rather than toil in the fields alongside her husband, delighting in this lucky upside to a broken arm. Papas Andreas was the last to arrive. As Spiros formally introduced us the solemnity of the moment was ruined by Maria launching into a tirade about how Andreas had forgotten to go round to take her rubbish to the bins. The Papas promised he would attend to it after the blessing, winking at me and leaning in to thank me for putting an end to his mother's disgusting habit of burning plastic.

Everyone gathered round the table of food as the Papas lit the candle, struggling to keep a straight face at the sight of the bunny. The Papas' rumbling stomach hinted he may be more interested in the food on offer than his apparently pseudo religious duty. Regaining his composure he poured water from a plastic bottle into the soup bowl, next dipping his gold cross into the water. Just in case I wasn't sure what was going on Spiros loudly informed me that the water was now miraculously holy. I considered this quite a remarkable feat since I recognised the water bottle as the type sold in bulk at Lidl. Next the Papas dipped his sprig of basil in the holy water and started intoning the trisagion prayer, shaking his sprig as we followed him from room to room. Our Greek guests recited the prayer along with the Papas, whilst the non-Greeks muttered incomprehensively under their breath, pretending they knew the words.

The moment the priest stopped praying everyone descended on the food like a committee of vultures. Spiros informed me all the evil spirits had been expunged from my home and everyone in it was now blessed. Papas Andreas attempted to hide his amusement when Kyria Maria called out to me, "You'll be glad to get rid of the spirit of Pedros," referring to Spiros' uncle whom she had been engaged in a two-decade feud with before he plunged from the roof of our house.

Whilst everyone was tucking into the buffet Eduardo the electrician turned up to wire the water tank up to the electricity. His arrival was a tad untimely, but I was prepared to put up with the inconvenience rather than anymore cold showers.

The feta and pickle sandwiches were met

with universal disgust, but the cressless egg and cress sandwiches went down a treat. Marigold's Greek cakes were such a success that all the Greek guests were convinced they must be shop bought, not expecting a foreigner to have mastered the subtleties of Greek baking so skilfully. The trifle proved such a delicious triumph that the bowl was soon empty; Marigold washed it out and poured the remainder of the holy water into it, embarrassed it had been left to sit in a humble soup bowl rather than cut glass.

Dina was in her element telling everyone about Kostis' upcoming marriage. Even though Kostis was yet to propose to Eleni, bringing her home to meet his parents was considered as good as an engagement. She clucked about what a good boy I was for coming to her help in the taverna, and revealed that I had volunteered to bake the bread for the whole village on Friday morning. The Greeks all tutted incredulously at this news, warning me I had bitten off more than I could chew.

"Only Dina still to bake by the old method Victor, it is too much the work, too much. If Dina not to bake for the village we would buy bread from the shop or make it in the modern machine like the one in your kitchen," Vangelis said.

"Well I'm quite looking forward to trying out the traditional method," I lied. The last thing I wanted to do was get up at four in the morning after toiling in the taverna until midnight, to bake bread in an outdoor oven, especially since I felt Nikos had somehow manipulated me into volunteering.

Marigold and I had agreed it was decidedly inappropriate to serve alcohol at a morning house blessing ceremony, so I put the kettle on to offer coffee to our guests. There was an enormous cracking sound, like thunder, accompanied by smoke spiralling out of the kettle. Eduardo the electrician stuck his head around the door, his hair standing on end, swearing in an apparent mix of Albanian and Greek. Spiros retorted in such quick fire Greek I couldn't catch a word until he translated for my benefit. "The Eduardo he say he told the Marigold not to put on the kettle when he to rewire the shower. He thought she to understand because she to smile and give him the cheese sandwich. I tell the blithering idiot the Marigold not to understand him to speak and the sandwich was to be the polite."

With no possibility of coffee the guests began

to take their leave. I noticed that Marigold, without any prompting from me, pressed Milton and Edna to take some of the leftovers home, refusing to take no for an answer. In that typically British way we all pretended the leftovers were for their cats, knowing in reality at least the elderly impoverished pensioners would not go hungry for the next few days. I was grateful Milton hadn't publicly embarrassed us by announcing in front of the priest he was penning a volume of erotica.

As Papas Andreas took his leave I thanked him for coming to bless the house with a short speech I had pre-prepared and memorised in Greek, enunciating the foreign words with as much solemnity as I could muster. The Papas stared at me hard, a look of confusion in his eyes, before creasing up with laughter and repeating my words for everyone to hear. The Greeks all exploded in laughter; it seemed I was the only one not in on the joke.

"Oh Victor, you need more the Greek lessons on the pronunciation," Spiros said. "Instead of to tell the Papas you thank him the much for the honour of blessing the house, you thank him for the honour of giving the house diarrhoea."

Chapter 10

Harold Repays Panos' Good Deed

The tour company Cynthia worked for was considering including the centuries-old town of Vathia, located in the Deep Mani, in their itinerary of day trips. This fortified settlement of crumbling tower houses mostly fallen to ruin perches atop a rugged and inhospitable landscape, high above the sea for protection against marauding pirates. I found the history of feuding families waging bloody vendettas against neighbouring clans and nailing the severed heads of their enemies on their walls, quite intriguing. Cynthia had been tasked with driving down to Vathia to take photographs for the tour company to display in their office.

As we cleared up the detritus of cake crumbs following the house blessing ceremony Cynthia announced she and Barry needed to leave since they were heading down to Vathia that afternoon. I must confess to turning green with envy since Vathia hadn't been ticked off my bucket list yet. Cynthia didn't seem too keen on my suggestion that I go along in place of Barry, even though I pointed out that having read up extensively on the history of the area I would be a more expert companion than my brother-in-law; Barry would likely be bored, viewing the ruins as something to be fixed up rather than appreciated for their rich history. I thought if I could impress Cynthia by filling in any gaps in her knowledge with pertinent facts, it might help to land me a position as a part-time tour guide during the summer. After all the taverna job was only temporary.

"Really Victor, you'll do anything to get out of the washing-up," Marigold scoffed, busily wrapping some leftover cake in tinfoil for them to take along on their trip. "Cynthia doesn't want to listen to you droning on, regurgitating dull facts from your history books; she wants a nice afternoon out with Barry."

"I could come along as well…" I began to say, only to be interrupted by Marigold saying, "Really Victor, you can be so obtuse at times, they don't want you tagging along like a gooseberry on their romantic trip out. Anyway there's no guarantee you'd be back in time for your shift in the taverna this evening and haven't you arranged to have coffee with that strange fellow who's always got his head buried in a book?"

"My afternoon rendezvous with Dimitris completely slipped my mind," I admitted shamefacedly.

"We can drive down to your ruins together one day soon," Marigold promised, alleviating the disappointment I felt from being excluded from the Vathia jaunt. Recognising I had been churlish by failing to appreciate Barry and Cynthia wanted time alone together away from the twitching curtains of the village I magnanimously suggested they take the Punto rather than Cynthia's rather unreliable second-hand run-around. Waving them off I reminded Barry to keep the windows wound down to alleviate any recurrence of his travel sickness and passed him a flask of the traditional vinegar and honey remedy as a precautionary placebo. I had added a dash of the holy water to the vile concoction; even though I was not convinced it was anything more than superstitious nonsense, I thought it couldn't do any harm.

As the Punto pulled away Panos pulled up in his tractor, towing a dented car in its wake. Ever since Panos first presented me with a gift of ripe grapes straight from his vine we had struck up as much of a friendship as two men struggling to understand each other could do. We shared a drink on occasion in the taverna and I had stopped by several times to admire Panos' grapevine and pick up some tips for establishing a vine around a trellis on the roof terrace. With the archaic and useless Greek phrase book replaced with a pocket-sized modern English to Greek dictionary we had managed to communicate with the odd word and a lot of gestures, and my Greek was beginning to improve to the extent that Panos and I could now enjoy the semblance of a chat.

Panos climbed down from the tractor cab, apologising profusely for missing the house blessing ceremony. He kept his Greek rudimentary enough for me to understand the gist of what he was saying as something along the lines of: 'Stupid British swimming pool Victor you must translate.' It was only then that I noticed a very dishevelled and overwrought Harold and Joan sitting in the tractor cab and realised it was their dented car that Panos was towing. Feeling quite smug that Panos considered me a suitable translator I waved for Harold to step down from the cab, thus subjecting myself to an onslaught of Greek in one ear from Panos and a litany of complaints in my other ear from Harold.

I noticed Harold's already reddened face was puce with the humiliation of needing my assistance, the irony not lost on him that a three-month newcomer to Meli was being called upon to translate for someone who'd lived out here for more than three years. I knew that as long as my Greek vocabulary extended beyond the word *beera* Harold would have no idea I was botching the language and confusing my tenses, clueless about anything I said. I indicated that Harold should keep quiet until I had listened to what Panos had to say. I managed to pick out odd words I was now familiar with, stringing them into a sort of sentence that sounded something like 'swimming pool drunk crazy car road ditch night help.'

Turning to Harold I said authoritatively, "I gather from Panos that you were driving home under the influence late last night and you managed to steer your car into a ditch. You're very fortunate that Panos towed it out instead of calling the police."

"Those bends are murder in the dark, is it any wonder I went off into a ditch when they can't be bothered to put any lights up. We were forced to spend a very uncomfortable night in the car because Joan was too frightened to walk back in the dark."

"It was quite impossible Harold, I had my heels on," Joan chimed in.

"Couldn't Harold have carried you?" I asked.

"We came off at the bottom of the hill; it's a good eight mile trek up here. Have you seen the size of Joan?" Harold said.

I didn't respond. I had seen quite enough of Joan's flab since she insisted on pouring it into a bikini whenever the weather permitted.

"You've no idea how horrid it was Victor, having to spend the night in the car. It was a complete nightmare, I thought we were going to be eaten by wolves; the constant howling sent shivers down my spine," Joan grumbled.

"Even if you are confusing wolves with jackals it is extremely unlikely you would find any in this area willing to eat you, they have been driven to near extinction according to a comprehensive survey conducted by the Greek World Wildlife Foundation. I could cite the latest statistics from 2000 if you're interested," I offered.

"We don't want to be bored silly with your stupid statistics; we want you to find out why this peasant didn't take the car to the garage like I told him to and call a taxi to bring us back home."

"I suppose he forced you into his tractor cab at gunpoint," I quipped sarcastically.

"Well no, but we weren't going to stay in the ditch while he made off with the car, he could be anyone for all we knew," Harold spluttered. "Next thing I know he'd be living rich from selling the parts for scrap."

"You have a nasty mind Harold, judging others by your own low standards. Can't you see that Panos has done you a favour towing your car up here, if it had been me I'd have left you to rot in the ditch? As you don't speak any Greek he couldn't understand you wanted to go to the garage, but he knew you lived in Meli.

Perhaps I should just ask Panos to tow you and the car back to where he found you and leave you to the mercies of whatever dog your ignorant wife mistook for a pack of wolves."

My last words were an angry bluff since I wasn't quite sure I had enough Greek to request Panos dumped them back in the ditch.

"*Ti, ti?*" Panos shouted, wanting to know what was being said and obviously picking up on my loss of temper.

"Don't do that, Joan can't take any more upset," Harold pleaded. "Just tell him to drop the car at the house."

"Tell him," I repeated indignantly, stretching myself to my full height all the better to look down on Harold. "I tell you what Harold; I won't tell him you just accused him of being the unsavoury sort who'd sell your car off for scrap and I'll consider not telling the local constabulary you were driving while two-sheets to the wind. Instead I'll tell Panos you'd be delighted to offer him fifty euros for his trouble. After all he went out of his way to help you and for his Good Samaritan act he missed our house blessing ceremony. He was very much looking forward to it, especially Marigold's sherry trifle."

"Yes of course, least I can do, don't go blabbing about what I said about scrap, just having a little joke," Harold blustered, reaching for his wallet, belatedly realising Panos might have a few years on him but would likely flatten him with one punch.

Turning back to Panos I told him the crazy swimming pool man wanted to pay him for his trouble. Panos insisted it wasn't necessary, but I insisted Harold wouldn't take no for an answer. Beaming with pleasure Panos promised he'd buy me a drink in the taverna that evening before climbing back in the tractor. As it pulled away I overheard Joan complaining "Did you hear that Harold, they had a party and didn't invite us."

"What was that all about Victor, please tell me you haven't been encouraging Harold," Marigold asked when I returned upstairs.

"Just bringing him down a peg with a bit of ritual humiliation," I assured her.

Chapter 11

Torturous Music

Even though I'd admittedly forgotten all about my arrangement to have coffee with Dimitris in the face of what I'd mistakenly thought was the better offer of a chance to visit Vathia, I had actually been looking forward to it. Dimitris' modestly studious air and polite manner led me to believe we may be kindred spirits.

Dimitris had prepared for our meeting by dragging a second hard backed chair onto his doorstep, thoughtfully providing a cushion for my comfort. He had just brewed a fresh *briki* of Greek coffee when I arrived; we shared our first moments in companionable silence sipping the strong bitter coffee, washing away the grinds that stuck in our teeth with a glass of cool water. Dimitris had piqued my curiosity since the moment we'd met in the shop, striking me as the solitary and scholarly type. I was not altogether surprised when Dimitris told me he had returned to the village of his birth following his retirement from his position as a professor of history at a university in Epirus; he had a professorial look about him.

"Nowhere in Greece is better than the Meli, I dream many year to return here, longing for the quiet of the village," Dimitris said.

"A man after my own heart, the peace of village life is very appealing," I agreed.

"It is much the different to your country Victor?"

"There's really no comparison between Meli and Manchester, of course village life is always different to city life," I replied.

"I have been back in Meli for one year now, since I took the early retirement," Dimitris told me. "I like the peace here very much, the city life not to suit me, the noise too much, everywhere the noise."

Dimitris' words confused me. By his appearance I had guessed he was in his early seventies, yet he spoke of taking early retirement the year before. I looked at him more closely, trying to gauge if I had presumptuously aged him in my mind. His pale skin lacked the typical weatherworn look shared by many of the village men. Working outdoors in the elements prematurely aged many of them, making them appear old beyond their actual years. Dimitris' shock of grey hair, whilst indicating age, was pulled back in an unflattering ponytail, perhaps a sign he was nostalgically clinging onto his lost youth. He was always smartly turned out in a tie, but the rest of his clothes had a dated air. The overall impression Dimitris conveyed was one of shabby neglect, befitting the image of the scholarly professor more interested in lofty philosophical thoughts than the more mundane things of life.

Sensing my scrutiny Dimitris turned to me, bluntly asking, "Tell me Victor, when you to look at me do you see the old man?"

"Well none of us are getting any younger," I hedged, "I'll be fifty-nine next month."

"Ah the same years, the coincidence is extraordinary, no wonder we feel the, how you say, sympatico. The difference is you look your age, I sadly look much the older," Dimitris sighed.

I wasn't sure if I'd understood him correctly; was he telling me he was only fifty-eight? I found it hard to believe; surely the professorial life was not one that would so visibly age a man beyond his actual years.

"I was born on December fourteenth 1944, that make me to be fifty-nine next month, sixty if you calculate by the Greek way of adding an extra year," Dimitris said. "And you Victor, you share the same birth month and year?"

"Yes, but I don't celebrate my birthday," I said flatly, my tone indicating I did not wish to elaborate. I hoped Dimitris was too much of a gentleman to press the matter. It was highly probable that Dimitris and I did indeed share the same birthdate, a remarkable coincidence if true, but one I had no hope of verifying. Although technically I must have an actual birth date, ambiguity surrounds it since my absconded parent neglected to bung a copy of my birth certificate in the bucket I was abandoned in. I have always refused to commemorate the date I was discovered abandoned in a bucket as

my actual birthday, considering it a far too ignominious start in life to celebrate. Although a
great one for birthdays, Marigold has always
humoured my express wish that the random
birthdate I was given is ignored. Since it is so
close to Christmas she gets round it by giving
me an extra pair of socks on the twenty-fifth.

Fortunately it appeared Dimitris was a tactful man, intuiting I did not wish to discuss the
subject further. Instead he broke the tension by
apologising for declining my invitation to the
house blessing ceremony, confessing he had invented the prior arrangement as a convenient
excuse.

"I cannot to stand the noisy gatherings Victor, it is a, how you say, the quirk of mine."

"I noticed you left the taverna very suddenly the other evening when Nikos started to
play the *bouzouki*," I said.

"Ah yes, the music is intolerable to me, I
cannot to stand it." Dimitris said. I bit back the
natural quip that Nikos' playing wasn't that bad
since I sensed it was more than Nikos' odd off-
key note that troubled Dimitris.

"It take me back to the island. Victor, you
will have heard of the island of Gyaros?" Dimitris asked, a look of pain evident in his eyes.

I pleaded ignorance, waiting for him to explain. Dimitris sighed heavily, saying, "So much the Greek history not known outside *Ellada*. Maybe it is the best forgotten, but I cannot to forget. You want I to tell?"

"Yes, but not if it stirs up bad memories for you," I replied, interested in what he had to say.

"The memories are always there, in every song on the radio, in every note of the *bouzouki*, even the jingle on the television advertisement flooding out to the street through open windows. What to do, the music is inescapable; it is part of the life, it is the most exquisite torture."

Dimitris divulged a harrowing tale. He was just twenty-three years old, a student of philosophy in Athens, when the Colonels' came to power in April 1967, establishing the military dictatorship of the junta. Unlike many of his contemporaries Dimitris was largely ignorant of politics, his head always buried in a philosophical tome. However he was not spared when the roundup of political dissidents began, presumed to be a communist for defiantly flouting the strict public ban on long hair.

"Imagine Victor, for my sin of vanity in refusing to cut my hair I was exiled to the prison island of Gyaros in the Aegean. For four months

I was tortured with the music thundering through loud speakers, there was no escape the noise, it much the worse than the physical torture. The *falanga* I could take, but the re-education music almost to drive me insane."

"Is the *falanga* a more bearable type of *rebetiko* music than the type they played as a re-education tool?" I asked.

"Oh Victor, you are such the innocent, the *falanga* is the name of the torture method where they beat the soles of the feet. Even as they cudgel the feet they blasted the Greek patriotic songs to cure the prisoners of the curse of communism; of course I was never a communist to be cured, being politically apathetic."

Dimitris' words made me wince at the thought of the suffering he had endured and at my own ignorance of these events.

"I suffer the *falanga*, I suffer the haircut, most of all I suffer the torturous music. Then suddenly they release me, they say mistake, I am not after all the communist. I never return to Athens or philosophy, I change to study history and keep out of the political argument, but see I am defiant and grow the hair long.. Now let us speak of more pleasant things. Today I have the good news; I am to be on the television."

Naturally I jumped to the conclusion Dimitris would be appearing in his professional capacity as a professor of history, to add some authority to a subject he was a specialist in.

"I take the bus to Athens tomorrow," Dimitris said.

"You must tell me when you're on and I'll tune in," I said.

"It will be *methavrio* on the Mega channel. Of course there is no the guarantee I will get in the hot seat, I have to first win the finger fastest first."

"The finger fastest first?" I queried thinking it sounded familiar.

"Yes, I must first to have the fastest finger to get on the hot seat of the 'Who Wants to be a Millionaire'," Dimitris revealed. I smiled at his words: each evening as I made my way to the taverna I could hear the familiar refrain of the theme music from the popular show washing into the street from behind shuttered windows, making me reflect its popularity was a common bond shared between our two cultures.

"Tell to me Victor, do you have any special knowledge in case I get the difficult question I cannot to answer? Do you have the enough knowledge to be the phone the friend?"

"I can certainly help you out if you get any tricky questions on food borne pathogens, dangerous contaminants, or health and safety regulations," I volunteered.

"That is excellent; I know nothing about these tedious subjects. Perhaps you would furnish your telephone number and help me to win the one hundred and fifty thousand euros if the pathogenic question comes up."

"Ah, you're taking the cautious approach and not aiming for the million," I noted. "A wise decision not to risk a sum you have already won, by gambling on a guess."

"There is no the million Victor, not since the euro came in. Last year the Giorgios Georgopoulos win the fifty million drachma, but now the top prize is in the euro and is just the one fifty. Spiros explain to me the rules and I have thought about the gamble and will to be happy with the ten thousand euro. I not knowledgeable about the pathogens, my area of expertise is in the history and philosophy. But now I have you to be the pathogen phone the friend, Papas Andreas is the religion phone the friend, and the Spiros is the movie phone the friend. He watch many the movie to learn the English."

"I will be proud to be your phone a friend,"

I assured him, proud indeed to have been selected to join such illustrious company as Spiros and Papas Andreas. It struck me he didn't have anyone ready to leap into the breach if a question on music came up, but perhaps his political re-education had that covered.

"You must come again Victor, we are I think the sympatico. Next time I teach to you to play the *tavli*."

Chapter 12

Victor Drugs Marigold with Cat Sedatives

Working until midnight in the taverna was beginning to play havoc with my regular up-with-the-lark daily routine. I was peeved to note that Barry had risen before me, claiming first dibs on the shower. As I sipped my first coffee and waited for him to finish his ablutions I was disturbed by a piercing scream emanating from the bathroom. Barry emerged in a towel with his hair standing on end, advising, "I really think you should find a more competent electrician, I was just electrocuted in the shower by Eduardo's incompetent wiring job."

After suffering yet another cold shower until the botched wiring could be fixed, I crushed some sedatives into Clawsome's food and took Marigold coffee in bed. Now she had safely delivered two mutant kittens we were taking Clawsome back to the veterinarian to finally be sterilised. It was too soon to get her kittens done, but the whole procedure would be repeated as soon as possible. I had no wish to be held responsible for increasing Meli's already rampant population of ferals.

Cynthia had absolutely refused my suggestion that she should have Kouneli, her ugly grey mutant Tom, neutered. I had argued with her to no avail, pointing out that her vile cat would be less aggressive, less inclined to mark its territory with indiscriminate spaying, and most importantly unable to unload its mutant genes on every tabby it indiscriminately ravished. Cynthia was adamant, saying, "I refuse to put my darling Kouneli through such a traumatic emasculating procedure. I'd like to see you offering to be voluntary castrated Victor."

Marigold had sent me one of her withering

looks as a warning that my vasectomy was a private matter between us and I should not risk it becoming village gossip by divulging this personal information to Cynthia.

Barry enthused about the trip to Vathia, promising to send me copies of the photographs he had taken once they were developed. He told me that they had braved the November water, taking a dip in the sea down at Porto Kagio before drying off on the beach. I made a mental note to give the car a quick going over with the hand-held vacuum before setting off for town, to avoid getting sand in my extremities.

Whilst I waited for Marigold to get ready I took another stroll around to Guzim's shed since he still hadn't put in an appearance. I was seriously beginning to suspect something amiss had happened to him and made a mental note to discuss with Spiros the difficulties of officially reporting the disappearance of an illegal. It wouldn't do for him to suddenly turn up, only to face deportation because of reckless meddling on my part.

It proved a struggle to get Clawsome into her basket. I forgave the inevitable scratches, surmising her sixth sense must have alerted her that we were off to the veterinarian. I made a mental note to ask the vet to prescribe a stronger cat sedative since it didn't appear to be working, Clawsome remaining playfully frisky despite the usual dosage. It was only when Marigold began snoring in the car on the road leading out of Meli that I realised in my exhausted state I had accidentally crushed the sedatives into my wife's coffee instead of the cat food. Fortunately a blast of fresh sea air when we hit the coast brought Marigold out of her drugged slumber. I decided it would be prudent to keep quiet about the mix up or I would likely never hear the end of it.

The ninety-minute drive to town gave us plenty of time to catch up. Marigold confessed she was beginning to miss my company in the evenings and I reminded her that it was she who had volunteered me to work in the taverna. She promised to come along the next evening when I told her that Nikos was bringing his television set to the taverna so everyone could watch Dimitris star in 'Who Wants to be a Millionaire.'

"As a professor he's bound to make it into the chair," Marigold said enthusiastically, impressed that I was friends with the village sage. She was excited that my voice may be broadcast throughout Greece if I received the telephone call from Spiros Papadopoulos, the host of the show, to say I was the selected phone a friend. Even though she always pretended to be above such tacky game shows I had caught her watching it on more than one occasion. I actually had my doubts that Dimitris would be fast enough on the finger round to get into the hot seat; it struck me that although Dimitris was learned in his chosen field he epitomised the image of the absent minded professor who would struggle with mundane tasks such as tying his shoelaces and hitting the buzzer.

I shared with Marigold the extraordinary coincidence that Dimitris and I could very well share an actual birthdate. She was relieved I hadn't blurted out to him the details of my ignominious start in life, worried that I would become the butt of bucket jokes if my early abandonment should ever get out. I reminded her it may be only a matter of time until the Violet Burke woman who had turned up at our Manchester address a month after our move, looking for her long lost son, tracked me down in Greece.

"We will deal with that if we have to Victor, but there's no point in worrying about her arrival unnecessarily. After all it's been two months since she turned up in Manchester and we haven't heard a dicky bird since."

Marigold remained convinced that the Burke woman may well be an imposter and insisted if she ever turn up that I demand a DNA test. I knew in my gut that Violet Burke was indeed the absconded parent and instead of being a Bucket I was most likely a Burke.

I suggested that Marigold should come along the next morning to lend a helping hand baking bread for the village, but she flatly refused, pointing out I had volunteered myself into that one and it couldn't be pinned on her.

"I have other plans anyway Victor; I have been invited to the house of another ex-pat for morning coffee. It will be a good opportunity to expand my social circle a little."

"Well don't limit new friendships to expats," I advised. "Your language skills will come along much more quickly if you socialise with the Greeks."

"Most of the Greeks we spend time with insist on speaking English," Marigold sighed. It was true that our closest friends, Spiros and Vangelis, were both eager to improve their English. Our language was a useful skill for Vangelis, securing him work in foreign houses, and

Spiros never knew if he would have to deal with an English corpse.

"That is why working at the taverna has turned into a blessing in disguise; I am forced to really try to get to grips with the language. When I started there I could barely understand a word Dina said but after being pushed together in the kitchen I can almost manage a conversation with her now. She was telling me last night how she can't wait for Kostis to be married so she can retire and let Eleni take over the drudge work; apparently it's the expected thing for the new bride to wait on her mother-in-law."

"I wonder if we could persuade Benjamin to take a Greek wife," Marigold pondered.

"Need I remind you that Benjamin is out and proud?" I reminded her.

"I just meant for show Victor, don't be so literal. A Greek daughter-in-law could produce a grandchild and do the drudge work around the house."

"You have me for that dear, and you don't need a grandchild now that we are overrun with kittens."

I suspected Marigold just wanted an excuse to buy a new hat; she does love a good wedding. I reminded my wife that Benjamin and Adam had become involved with a group petitioning for gay marriage. "Mark my words Marigold, on some not too distant day in the future you will wear a new hat when the boys get married."

"Oh Victor, you do have the knack of saying just the right thing sometimes. I will come along with you in the morning to give you a hand with the bread, before my coffee date," Marigold offered. I was touched by her offer, even though I knew it would take an earthquake to get Marigold out of bed at four in the morning.

Marigold told me she'd spent the previous evening running up my phone bill on a long distance call to Geraldine, her best friend back in England. The two of them had worked together, retaining a close friendship in spite of the incident that resulted in Marigold's unexpected resignation from her position as a pet food taster.

"Poor Geraldine is feeling rather down. Her latest boyfriend has just dumped her in the most callous way possible," Marigold said.

"How unfortunate," I said, politely humouring my wife since I have zero interest in Geraldine's convoluted love life. "Did it involve public humiliation?"

"Oh much worse than that, he dumped her by email, can you imagine a more wimpish way to go about things, not even the courtesy of telling her in person. The cowardly milksop has obviously been emasculated by the over saturation of fluoride in the water supply."

Sometimes I wonder if Marigold ever thinks before she prattles or if she even pays attention to my lengthy diatribes concerning hygiene. Surely she must be aware that I am a staunch supporter of water fluoridation as an excellent method of preventing cavities across mass populations. There has never been any evidence that synthetic fluoride leads to unmanly behaviour, even though toxicology compendiums technically label it a neurotoxin.

My thoughts distracted by fluoride, I had tuned out, but suddenly tuned back into Marigold's prattling when I heard the words, "So of course I told Geraldine she must come and stay with us, some winter sunshine is just what she needs to cheer her up. Luckily she managed to get a last minute flight to Athens this Sunday. We must introduce her to all the eligible bachelors we know, a handsome Greek man could be just the tonic she needs. Oh for heaven's sake Victor, don't pull that face, she's only staying for a week."

I had hoped that by insisting we made an early start to town we would avoid the waiting room saga at the veterinarian's office. Arriving just after nine proved to be of no advantage since the waiting room was already packed with animals and their owners. The leather clad tattooed motorcyclist who spoke excellent English was there once again with his pampered pet poodle Fufu. It was gratifying to see he recognised us, immediately shuffling up to make room for us.

"I thought we'd avoid the wait by arriving early," I told him.

"Everyone has the same idea; there was a scrum on the doorstep waiting for him to open. Today I am next after the parrot and one before the goat," he said. "I think to suggest he introduce the ticket system, that way we could all claim a ticket and go off for coffee."

"Like they do at the bank," I observed.

"Indeed yes, but I was thinking of the hospital," the motorcyclist said.

"Surely they operate an appointment system at the hospital," I said in surprise.

"Certainly they do, but they give everyone the same appointment time and the ticket is claimed on arrival. Let me advise you how you must handle the hospital," he said, leaning in close to whisper, "You must to arrive the two-hour before the appointment to take the ticket, and then you can go off for coffee until the ticket desk opens."

"Let's hope we don't need the hospital then, we have to come into town all the way from Meli so it would mean leaving in the middle of the night to get here to grab one of the first tickets to avoid waiting around all day," Marigold said.

"Let me advise you another way," the helpful motorcyclist hissed. "Better to use the nepotism, find someone in Meli who has a connection to someone who works at the hospital, it can be anyone from the surgeon to the cleaner. They can meet you at the ticket desk and walk you past everyone who is waiting and take you straight into the doctor."

"But surely that's queue jumping," I protested.

"It would be, but as you know we don't have the queuing system in Greece. Personally I have the luck to have my mother's neighbour's second cousin twice removed working at the hospital as a phlebotomist so I can barge right in. You must to find out if you have a Meli hospital contact."

"Our friend Spiros is an undertaker," I said.

"Excellent, excellent, no doubt he will have a useful connection you can use in the mortuary. So you live in Meli, a lovely village, you are very lucky."

"Yes, we are," we agreed.

"Sometimes I like to ride out that way on the motorbike; I have a special basket attached for Fufu."

Although I would have loved to delve into motorcycle regulations and discover why so many motorcyclists insisted on wearing their helmets on their arms instead of their heads, our friendly leather clad companion was called in by the vet, overtaking the parrot that was sup- posedly next up. I sent a warning look to the miniature Maltese that was next in after Claw- some; I didn't want it getting any ideas it could usurp our turn.

Chapter 13

Pig Swill

After yet another late night hovering over the heat of the deep fat fryer and pouring copious amounts of extra virgin olive oil over salads I had chucked together, I was not amused when the alarm roused me at four o'clock the next morning. It was too dark to see what the weather was up to, but the sound of the plastic chairs flying around on the roof top terrace led me to believe it was a tad windy. I was very grateful for the railings Vangelis had installed around the roof; it wouldn't go down well if one of the plastic chairs was to fly off the roof terrace and put a passing villager in a coma.

Creeping from the bed so as not to disturb Marigold I headed into the kitchen in search of strong coffee. The only advantage of being up well before the lark was I could claim first dibs on the hot water since there was no sign of Barry. I suspected his room was empty. Barry had most likely snuck out to spend the night with Cynthia, though he would never think to besmirch her reputation by admitting it. If the guest room was indeed empty it would solve the dilemma of where to put Geraldine when she arrived on Sunday. Marigold was reluctant to turf her brother out of the spare bedroom and make him bed down on the sofa bed in my office, but equally reluctant to expect Geraldine to sleep next to the shredder. I hoped my wife wasn't harbouring any ridiculous notions of converting our downstairs storage into a guest suite.

Even after two strong coffees I was in no mood to venture out into the cold dark morning to bake bread in a traditional outdoor Greek bread oven, even with two pullovers under my wax jacket. The weather was very changeable, confusing with the pretence of summer on days with sunshine and high temperatures, followed by bursts of torrential rain and winds strong enough to lift me off my feet. Still, weather wise it was an improvement on Manchester's relentless grey drizzle. Forcing myself outdoors I was amazed by how different the village appeared at this unnatural hour, the olive trees eerily rattling their branches in tune to the wind, no feral cats to trip over since they were so thoroughly bedded down in doorways or sleeping under the bins. I almost lost my footing when a stray carrier bag lifted by the wind slapped me full in the face, no doubt blown there from the bins. Perhaps Kyria Maria had known a thing or two after all with her obsession for burning plastic.

A light was on in the apartment above the taverna where Dina and Nikos lived. It was unusual to see any sign of life from up there since the pair of them were either toiling in the fields during the day or toiling away in the taverna until past midnight. They had remarkable stamina for their age, something Nikos credited to avoiding all shop bought rubbish and lining his stomach with a glass of extra virgin olive oil before pouring the *spitiko*.

Dina opened the taverna door to greet me, hardly recognisable beneath the random dusting of flour coating her from head to toe. She ushered me inside, insisting I warm up by the *somba* which she had stoked into life from the previous night's embers. She presented me with a strong Greek coffee she had taken the liberty of sweetening with half a bag of sugar, rendering it completely undrinkable.

Two of the taverna tables had been pushed together and covered in flour ready for punching the dough down; two large sacks of flour standing open on the floor hinting this could turn into a mammoth production line. By the time I had made quick work of the toasted bread drizzled with olive oil and speckled with oregano that Dina forced on me, she had already thrown the first batch of dough on the table, ready for me to start punching and kneading. This stage was beyond her with her arm in plaster, but she fussed over me, directing my pummelling and apologising that I had been dragged out of bed to help her. I soon found my bread kneading rhythm, alternately imagining the dough I was punching was Harold or the featureless Violet Burke person.

We seemed to have been at it for hours but it was still barely light when Nikos came downstairs, kissing his wife affectionately and ribbing me that I had a natural bent for the women's work. Knocking back a strong sweet coffee he collected the kitchen scraps left over from the previous evening to feed to the pigs, making me grateful pork hadn't been on the grill since I would hate to see Nikos tempting his swine into cannibalistic practices. I wasn't sure if the 2001 ban on feeding pig swill to pigs, prompted by the recent outbreak of foot and mouth disease, was applicable in Greece, though it was an EU directive. I made a mental note to do some re-search on this fascinating subject.

"Come early tonight to peel extra potatoes Victor, I expect to be busy. Many the people will come to watch the Dimitris on the television," Nikos reminded me before roaring off on his moped for a day in the fields. Dina told me that Nikos would be starting his olive harvest within the next two weeks and she didn't think she would be much use without her arm. She must have spotted the look of alarm on my face that I was about to be volunteered to help with the harvest because she creased up with laughter, telling me not to worry, Nikos could hire the Guzim to take her place. This did little to reas-sure me I wouldn't be roped in since Guzim was still on the missing list.

I was not looking forward to venturing out into the cold again to light a fire in the outside bread oven, expecting it to be a tricky process with the wind howling. I was surprised when Dina told me she had already lit the fire before I arrived, since the fire needed to die down to embers to create the right temperature for baking. As I kneaded and Dina fussed I attempted to explain the concept of mulled wine, saying I imagined it would be a popular addition to serve hot spicy wine in the taverna on cold evenings. Even though she made polite noises I could tell Dina considered the concept a foreign aberration; nevertheless I promised to bring along a stock of my own personal spices that evening to demonstrate.

I was just wondering how to dispose of the latest sweet coffee without offending Dina when the taverna was invaded by a gaggle of elderly Greek ladies, all aproned up ready to give Dina a hand with the bread baking. Cackling with laughter at the sight of me doing women's work, they told me I was a good boy for volunteering but they'd take over from here. Apparently there had never been any question that Dina would not have the assistance of the village ladies for the important ritual of Friday bread baking; it had been Nikos' little joke to drag me into it. Their arrival stirred conflicting feelings within me; on the one hand I was very grateful that Dina had the full support of the village ladies and I could now make a welcome exit. On the other hand, in a rather perverse way, I would have liked to see the job through. A compromise was suggested and I agreed to return at noon to watch the first loaves being pulled from the oven.

It was a relief to know that the next few hours would be my own. Marigold was off out visiting and Barry was sure to be at Cynthia's place. I debated between penning a chapter or two of my book about moving to Greece or spending some time reading up on the latest hygiene regulations just in case Dimitris managed to get in the hot seat that evening. Even though all the odds were stacked against my receiving the phone a friend call relating to germs or pathogens, I would never live down the public humiliation if I fluffed the help he needed in my role of a phone the friend. I decided I would treat myself to a bit of research on the latest pig swill regulations; if nothing else it would be useful to be armed with the latest facts when I confronted Nikos. It was time he learned that feeding scraps to his swine was a filthy habit he must curb.

Dina insisted on loading me up with three giant loaves of fresh heavenly bread browned from the outdoor embers when I returned to proudly watch the loaves emerge from the oven. Litsa, the old lady who lived opposite the taverna, had very kindly prepared a large dish of boiled horta for me to take home, the wild green leaves that are a Greek favourite served with a generous squeeze of fresh lemon. Marigold was delighted to find lunch waiting for her on the table on her return from the coffee morning.

"I'm sure we are going to derive many benefits from eating so healthily," she said. "I would never imagine weeds could be so tasty, but this horta is delicious."

"In addition to being a rich source of vitamins," I added.

I was glad that Marigold could appreciate such simple fare; I had long worried that her work as a pet food taster would play havoc with her taste buds.

"Do you think we should plant some horta in the garden?" Marigold asked.

"We don't need to plant weeds, they grow wild all over the place, we simply have to forage for them," I pointed out. We could often see the elderly ladies of the village foraging for horta and wild asparagus, though as yet we had not been tempted to join them.

"But I don't want people to get the wrong idea and think we can't afford to buy food," Marigold said.

"I'm sure people would make allowances since it's pretty much general knowledge that Nikos is only paying me three euros an hour," I laughed. "How did your morning coffee go?

"Very well. It was nice to meet Doreen, she seems very pleasant. Her husband Norman was a bit of a bore, he blended into the background like nondescript wallpaper. Doreen hasn't got your magic touch with a lemon drizzle though, it was quite flat and decidedly unlemony. She warned me that I might get sick of Greek food before long; it reminded me of you getting all tzatzikied out. We discussed starting a monthly dining club where we each take it in turns to cook and host a foreign meal, she's going to ask around and see if she can drum up much interest. I'm sure your Indian cooking would make quite an impression Victor, and we have enough spices to make it authentic."

"You don't spend as much time in Indian kitchens as I did during my illustrious career as a health inspector without picking up on a few finer points of the cuisine," I said smugly.

"Apparently Cynthia's toad-in-the-hole is quite famous amongst the ex-pats, though seemingly they aren't all too keen on having a single woman along, they say it messes up the seating arrangements," Marigold prattled on. I hoped the reluctance to include Cynthia wasn't down to Harold's fabricated gossip that she was a loose floozy.

"I expect that once it becomes public knowledge that Cynthia is walking out with Barry they'll be keener to include her," Marigold said, implying the other ex-pat women would feel their husbands would be safe from Cynthia's presumed advances if they knew she was spoken for. I wondered if I really wanted to be dragged into an ex-pat social whirl, no doubt relegated to conversing with the boring Norman. I considered perhaps I was turning Greek, preferring the companionable friendships I was establishing with the Greek men of Meli I was learning to converse with. Marigold seemed rather keen on extending our social circle of

British couples, but it held little appeal to me as an avowed European. It struck me as shallow to form convenient friendships based on nothing more than a common language. Nevertheless I would no doubt go along with my wife for a quiet life, doomed to spend evenings playing one-upmanship, discussing house prices and complaining one simply couldn't get quality teabags in Greece.

"I suppose Barry is off somewhere with Cynthia. Whilst he's out I need you to give me a hand changing his sheets and making up his bed for Geraldine," Marigold said, scuppering my plans for a pleasant afternoon spent researching the hazards of pig swill.

"I rather think he's been spending his nights with Cynthia," I said.

"Well of course he has, he's been sneaking out as soon as I've gone to bed and then sneaking back in at first light," Marigold winked. "I'll have to tactfully suggest he moves onto the sofa bed in your office, without letting him know we know he's not been sleeping here at all."

"Why on earth should we keep up the ridiculous pretence, he's a grown man after all. Are we meant to be so prudish that we'd be shocked? And as we both know he's been sleeping at Cynthia's why do we need to bother changing his sheets for Geraldine?" I demanded.

"We must humour their charade to protect Cynthia's reputation, and the sheets must be changed because Barry has been encouraging the new kittens to bed down in there, you know how Geraldine feels about cats," Marigold said, reminding me of Geraldine's ailurophobia. I had always considered it odd that a woman that taste tests cat food for a living should have an irrational fear of cats. "I'll leave it to you to break the news to Barry that he must pretend to move onto the sofa bed in your office."

Chapter 14

Phone the Friend

T he pockets of my wax jacket were stuffed with cinnamon sticks, star anise and nutmeg, cloves and ginger powder. I arrived at the taverna for my evening shift with all the ingredients I needed to prepare a vat of mulled wine, hopefully before Nikos put in an appearance and discovered what I was up to. The wind hadn't abated so hot wine would surely be very welcome against the chill. For once Nikos was there before me, fiddling with the television aerial and attempting to tune into

Mega.

"It is no good Victor, I think it must be snowing in Athens," Nikos lamented, staring at the snowy screen displaying nothing but rotating horizontal lines.

"You just haven't got a good reception," I suggested. "What was the picture like upstairs?"

"You think I have the time to watch the television Victor? Kostis watch it, he never mention the strange lines."

"I'll give Barry a call if you like, he's very handy at fixing things," I offered, leaving Nikos thumping the ancient television as I made my way into the kitchen to tackle the potato mountain.

Fortunately Barry came to the rescue quite quickly. After tinkering with a few wires the television presented an almost snow free picture. Nikos grouped the chairs around the set, deciding he wouldn't fire up the grill until after Dimitris' television appearance. Luckily he still had to prepare the meat, leaving Barry and I alone in the kitchen. Relegating Barry to the role of kitchen skivvy, I put him in charge of peeling whilst I prepared a large pan of mulled wine. With any luck the smell of aromatic spices might disguise the prevailing smell of fried chips.

"I've been meaning to have a word Barry," I began tentatively, wishing Marigold hadn't landed me with her dirty work. "Marigold's friend Geraldine is arriving for a visit on Sunday and we need you to give up your bed for her. You don't mind taking the sofa bed in my office?"

"Oh spare me from that man-mad harpy. I'll take your office if you let me fix a lock on the door," Barry said, rolling his eyes. Unfortunately Barry had been a target of Geraldine's interest in the past. On a life mission to snag herself a new husband she wasn't too choosy, propositioning anything with a pulse. She was a pleasant enough woman, just a tad over eager to relinquish her single status.

"Of course you'd be at a much safer distance from Geraldine if you stayed over at Cynthia's place," I innocently suggested, continuing the ludicrous charade he wasn't already doing that in the first place.

"Oh, I couldn't possibly hurt Marigold's feelings like that, you know how she loves having me about the place and she's promised faithfully that she'll let Geraldine know I'm spoken for now," Barry said. "I've only got another few days before I have to get back to England, work calls. I'm really going to miss Cynthia when I leave, I think she could be the one."

"Well you'll just have to make a point of coming over to Greece more often," I suggested. "You know you're always welcome."

"Just not in the best spare bedroom," Barry replied with good humour.

The taverna was beginning to fill up with villagers eager to watch one of their own make his mark on the television. Dina came into the kitchen, wordlessly investigating the pan of simmering wine before scurrying outside to complain to her husband that the foreigner was up to odd things in her kitchen. Nikos dashed in, sniffing the contents of the pan suspiciously and demanding to know what nonsense I was up to now.

"I thought the regulars would appreciate trying something different Niko, this is mulled wine, it is very popular in winter."

"Mulled wine. What has the wine got to ponder, grapes are not well the known for their intellect," Nikos snapped. "Victor, when you volunteered to help out I said nothing about you to change the menu and introduce your fancy foreign things. The Greek food is the best in the world, I think the British food not have the good reputation the same."

"Mulled wine is a popular drink across Europe, it originated with the Romans," I explained. "It is simply red wine infused with spices and heated up."

"Phhh, what did the Romans know, the Ancient Greeks were first and did not need to put the shop bought rubbish into wine," Nikos blustered.

"Just taste it," I pleaded.

"Okay, I try it later when it cools down," he said reluctantly, rather missing the point of hot wine. "Don't go giving it to the customers Victor; they want my *spitiko*, not wine you have messed with, filling it with dreck from the shop."

"It sounds as though it will be just us two, Marigold and Cynthia on the mulled wine," Barry laughed. "We should be in for a good night; you've made plenty of it."

"I can't understand why Nikos is so unreasonable and unwilling to try new things," I complained.

"He runs a spit and sawdust Greek taverna and he serves what he knows and what his customers like. He doesn't want to turn it into something it isn't," Barry reasoned. "You wouldn't like it if he'd just marched into one of the kitchens you'd inspected and started telling you it would be a better practice to clean with vinegar rather than bleach."

"The idea of Nikos giving cleaning tips is simply preposterous," I countered. Ladling two large measures of mulled wine for us, I conceded Barry had a point. I considered it might not be such a good idea to lecture Nikos on feeding swill to the pigs, he'd definitely think I was overstepping my mark since my only experience of actual pig farming was theoretical.

"Ladle some more wine Victor, Cynthia and Marigold have arrived," Barry ordered. "At least we can enjoy it; it has a fabulous spicy kick. Is that star anise I can taste?"

"*Ela* Victor, '*Poios Thelei Na Ginei Ekatommyriouchos*' is on," Nikos called out in a friendly way, showing there were no hard feelings.

"That's a bit of a mouthful, could you understand him?" Barry asked, obviously impressed that my Greek was coming along.

"I'd hazard a guess that he just said 'Who Wants to be a Millionaire' is starting," I replied, not exactly difficult to translate since the familiar theme tune was a bit of a giveaway.

Barry and I joined the clump of villagers huddled round the television set, eagerly watching to see the camera pan over Dimitris. A cheer went up when the village professor waved nervously for the camera. Unfortunately, when the question was posed to the ten contestants competing to see who had the fastest finger, I was unable to understand it.

"He's got it, it's a question on dates in the history," Nikos shouted across to me, giving me the thumbs up. "Not such the simple question, Dimitris will walk it, he's very the clever."

Another resounding cheer filled the taverna when Dimitris was revealed to have placed the four dates in the correct order faster than any of the other contestants. He wasn't particularly quick but his accuracy paid off, with four of the other contestants speedily selecting the wrong order.

"Panos says he hopes Dimitris remembers to get the autograph of the host Spiros Papadopoulos," Nikos translated for my benefit.

Dimitris had only just sat down in the hot seat when the inevitable adverts came on. Greek television advertisement breaks were one of several frustrating things we'd encountered in Greek life, interrupting programmes at crucial moments, most typically two minutes before the end of a film. They also dragged on for so long that it was possible to cook a three-course meal before the programme resumed.

Nikos came over to me, saying, "Victor I apologise for being the so ungracious about the wine, please to give me some. Dina tell me you work very hard this morning with the bread. Soon I must to start the olives. It will be very the difficult without Dina to help, but without her arm it is impossible, imagine if she were to fall off the ladder again and lose the other arm."

I wasn't falling for it: did I really look as though I had 'gullible mug' plastered all over my face? There was no way I was going to let Nikos manipulate me into volunteering for a full day of olive picking before an evening shift in the taverna. Passing Nikos a glass of mulled wine I simply said, "*Yamas*," wondering if his pseudo-grovelling would make him receptive to my unwanted advice on pig swill.

The advert break was interminable; by the time the show resumed I was on my second glass of potent mulled wine and Marigold had taken advantage of the pause to collar me in the kitchen with her brilliant idea. She had decided to introduce our soon-to-be houseguest

Geraldine to as many eligible Greek bachelors as I could round up and invite to a dinner party on Monday evening. Apparently it would cheer her up after being dumped.

"But I will be working here on Monday evening, along with every other evening for the foreseeable," I countered.

"You can come in during the afternoon to do your prep Victor and we can have our dinner party at seven. You don't need to start here until nine," Marigold said.

"But the Greeks don't eat dinner so early," I pointed out.

"You must simply tell them it is our custom or explain they have to come early because you need to be here later on," Marigold reasoned. "I can't see Spiros turning down an invitation to meet an attractive English woman, you know how he thinks he's god's gift to tourist women."

"I would hardly describe Geraldine as attractive. Do you expect me to lie to Spiros?" I retorted.

"How can you be so churlish Victor, of course Geraldine is a very striking woman, she's just not your cup of tea. Anyway Spiros isn't exactly an oil painting himself, despite his delusions. Make sure you invite your new friend

Dimitris; you say he speaks English and Geraldine might consider him quite a catch. After all he's not nearly as old as he looks; though he'd look a lot better if I could get my scissors on his absurd ponytail."

"He will indeed be a great catch if he walks off with the winnings tonight," I admitted. "But Dimitris doesn't like noisy gatherings."

"It's a refined dinner party Victor, not a disco. If it gets too much for Dimitris I can always lend him my ear plugs," Marigold argued. "Now who else can your rope in? You must know some more single men."

"Litsa's brother is a widower, will he do?" I asked.

"Can't you take this seriously Victor, he's the one who's always eating raw garlic and he must be his mid-eighties," Marigold said dismissively, adding a withering look to her comment.

"He's still got a pulse," I said. "Is Panos past it too in your eyes or will he cut muster? I do enjoy his company."

"Well he has got an expensive tractor, invite him, and see if you can't find anyone else too who is eligible before Monday."

"And I suppose you'd like me to take charge

of the cooking?" I asked sarcastically.

"Oh, would you dear, that is so thoughtful of you to volunteer," Marigold gushed, my sarcasm having flown over her head.

"*Ela* Victor, '*Poios Thelei Na Ginei Ekatommyriouchos*' is back," Nikos called, beckoning for me to return to the hub clustered around the television.

The camera zoned in on Dimitris sweating nervously in the hot seat, looking every inch the nutty professor. The host's attempts at conversation, meant to put him at ease, met with only monosyllabic responses so Spiros Papadopoulos moved swiftly onto the first monetary question. There was a cumulative cheer when Dimitris correctly identified the olive as the national tree of Greece. It came as no surprise to the audience of taverna watchers that Dimitris had to ask the audience who won the 2000 world cup in order to bag two-hundred euros, as football was obviously far beneath my learned friend's radar; I must confess I too was clueless to the answer. He was forced to go fifty-fifty on the five-hundred euro question since he could hardly be expected to know the popular Eurovision Greek entry 'Die for You' was performed by Antique; it hadn't been part of the re-education music blasted in the prison camp. The taverna customers were suitably impressed when I screamed the correct answer at the television set, ignorant that I was word perfect in the lyrics following my road trip to Thessaloniki in Vangelis' van.

"They must to ask him the more difficult questions, Dimitris cannot be expected to know this simple stuff," Nikos shouted. "He is the intelligent man; they must to ask him about the philosophy or ancient poets."

Fortunately for Dimitris the next set of questions were a tad more highbrow. He sailed through with the correct answers, emphatically confident, before the interruption of the next advert break. When the show resumed Dimitris would be facing question ten, worth five-thousand euros.

"He only have the one life-line left," Spiros cried, wondering if he was about to receive the telephone call. "I hope he to save it for the question on the movie."

"I pray his question is about religion," Papas Andreas intoned.

"I just hope I've kept up to date with all the latest microorganism infections in case something pathogenic comes up and I am needed to save the day," I said.

Spiros sidled over to me whilst the adverts played, saying he was very much looking forward to dining at my home on Monday, even if I did insist on feeding him in the middle of the afternoon. "Marigold say she have the attractive tourist friend to visit, maybe I get lucky," Spiros said with a broad wink.

"A wink should do the trick," I laughed. "Geraldine is a man-eater."

"I hope your English food is as good as the wine, this hot drink is most excellent," Spiros whispered, looking around to ensure Nikos was out of earshot before adding, "But don't to tell the Nikos I say so."

"*Ela* Victor, '*Poios Thelei Na Ginei Ekatommyriouchos*' is on again, hurry not to miss it," Nikos called out above the familiar refrain of the theme tune. We all gathered in a huddle around the television set once again, waiting with bated breath to see if Dimitris knew the answer to question ten. Once again I couldn't make head or tail of the question since the presenter's Greek was a tad too fast for my modest translating skills to cope with, but there was a collective sigh as the taverna regulars all agreed it was a difficult one. The camera zoomed in on a droplet of sweat trickling down from Dimitris' receding hairline, then rolling down his nose. I caught the words "*tilefono o filos,*" and turned to stare at the antiquated old telephone Nikos kept in the taverna. As the phone began to ring Nikos rushed to answer it, only to be shouted down by all the locals telling him to stop, the call was for Victor, but the question was very difficult.

Hoping I had not knocked back too much mulled wine to answer coherently I picked up the receiver. It was strange to have the host of the show I could see on the television talking into my ear. Luckily Dimitris must have told him I was English and Spiros Papadopoulos greeted me in my own language, telling me he had my friend Dimitris in the hot seat and perhaps I could help him out.

Dimitris' voice simultaneously came out of the television and down the telephone receiver.

"Victor, what type of virus led to the outbreak of foot and the mouth disease confirmed in the Greece in July 2000. Was it Australia 1, Asia 1, Europe 1, or Antarctica 1?"

"It was Asia 1, Dimitri, one-hundred percent," I announced authoritatively.

"You are the sure Victor? It is the lot of money."

"I'm positive Dimitri, it was Asia 1."

"Thank you my friend."

"Ask him if he's free for dinner on Monday," Marigold piped up, just as the phone line went dead.

Without any hesitation Dimitris confidentially declared the correct answer was Asia 1. The host attempted to confuse him by asking if he was sure he wanted to gamble, but Dimitris was resolute, saying, "*telikos apandisi.*" A roar of applause went up when it was confirmed it was indeed the correct answer just as the familiar theme tune blasted through the taverna yet again.

Nikos subjected my upper back to a hearty slap, telling me, "You know the most peculiar things, who could possibly have the interest in the viruses?"

"It's a fascinating subject," I replied. "Perhaps we could have a chat about your pig swill later."

"Of course Victor, when we chat about the olive harvest," Nikos responded. I made a mental note to stay out of Nikos' way for the rest of the evening. I refused to allow him to take advantage of my slightly intoxicated state to have me volunteering myself to help with his olive harvest.

Everyone was on tenterhooks when the programme resumed. Dimitris was facing question eleven, worth a whopping ten thousand euros. Alas popular culture reared its ugly head once again to confront Dimitris with a question about which actor played James Bond in 1986. A collective groan went round the taverna; Dimitris only kept a television to watch historical documentaries. Spiros screamed his answer at the television, lamenting, "The Dimitris should have to saved his phone the friend for this question."

"But he wouldn't have even seen this question if he hadn't phoned Victor about the last one," Barry argued. "Anyway Dimitris won't lose anything if he guesses this one and gets it wrong, he'll still go home with the five thousand."

"Phhh, he should have guessed the virus," Spiros scoffed. "I should have gone on instead of the Dimitris, I know all the answer except the virus and I could have to phoned Victor to be the friend. How Dimitris could be so the stupid to not know the Eurovision answer?"

Litsa's brother Matthias, the garlic eating pensioner, muttered something that seemed to rile everyone up. I fired a quizzical look at Spiros who obligingly translated, "The old man say what can you to expect from a communist? I tell him this is the baseless accusation and the professor is not political."

Nikos banged the table demanding everyone pipe down. Dimitris was about to gamble on the ten thousand euro question. Dimitris toyed with the options, tentatively plumping for David Niven. Spiros' shout of "*lathos,*" meaning wrong, nearly deafened me. Since I was personally clueless to the identity of any James Bonds other than Roger Moore I shushed Spiros, waiting to see if Dimitris had given the correct answer.

"He is the wrong Victor, David Niven play the spoof Bond, everyone to know that," Spiros yelled. "It was the very good movie."

Alas Spiros was proved to be correct; Dimitris had opted for the wrong Bond. Dimitris didn't seem too bothered; he just appeared very relieved of the chance to escape from the hot seat, clutching his five thousand euros.

"You did well Victor, without you he would have left with nothing," Barry said.

Flushed with pride or possibly too much mulled wine, I accepted the congratulations of the taverna goers for my sterling performance as a phone the friend. Everyone agreed Dimitris had put up a pretty feeble performance for a professor and without my help he would have gone home with nothing, out of pocket since he'd shelled out on the bus fare to Athens.

As a token gesture Barry offered to fry the chips whilst I basked in my success.

Chapter 15

A Gift from Albania

Since the Millionaire celebrations carried on long past midnight, toasted with copious amounts of mulled wine, I decided to treat myself to the unheard of luxury of a lie-in the next morning. Alas, it was not to be. It was barely first light when pounding on the front door disturbed me from my slumbers, the sound so loud it even woke Marigold who sleepily complained, "Who on earth decides to come calling at such an intolerable hour, do get rid of them Victor." I lay there for another thirty seconds, pointlessly wishing Barry had snuck back from Cynthia's house at dawn and might be on hand to open the door.

I was taken aback to discover the elusive Albanian, Guzim the shed dweller, standing on the doorstep, looking his usual shabby self and flashing his almost toothless smile. I was genuinely relieved to see he was actually alive rather than pushing up daisies under the shed. It seemed I had rather let my imagination run away with me and I was glad I had not drawn attention to his questionable immigration status by reporting his disappearance to the police. I couldn't recall how many days exactly he'd been on the missing list. The last time I'd seen him he'd been carousing and brawling in my garden with the Albanian chap he'd sold my shirt to. In the circumstances my greeting was understandably brusque; Guzim's shenanigans in my garden had been an uncouth display and his disappearance had after all inconvenienced my gardening schedule. On the other hand Guzim's reappearance might put an end to Nikos' hints that I should volunteer to help him with the olive harvest, since he could now hire the Albanian.

In his gutturally accented Greek Guzim

informed me he had just returned from Albania and was a father. As I already knew he was a father I felt it had been a tad unnecessary to wake me up with this momentous non-news. Guzim launched into a fast paced gushing monologue which made no sense, beaming broadly as he spewed every syllable. Catching my hint that he needed to slow down he began again, puncturing his now exaggeratedly slow speech with animated gesticulations. Thinking I had a grasp on his meaning I said *"Echete ena agori?"* asking him if he'd a boy. Guzim confirmed that after three girls he was finally the proud father of a baby boy. As soon as he'd received the news he had headed back to Albania to celebrate this momentous event; 'tellingly' he wouldn't have bothered making the trip if it turned out he'd fathered a fourth girl.

Guzim said that my obsession with Fatos Nano, the prime minster of his country, had made him realise the esteemed politician whom he'd previously despised had put Albania on the map. He had not expected Fatos Nano to be so famous in foreign parts so far away as my great country of Great Britain, but he was so impressed that he had named his first son Fatos in his honour. I didn't have the heart to tell him that I'd never heard of Fatos Nano until I'd used the useless phrase 'your prime minister is very handsome,' to practice my Greek from my archaic phrase book. Fortunately the Greek I was picking up in the taverna and with my new friends meant I didn't need to use the obsolete phrase anymore, a great relief since it had led to the embarrassing misunderstanding that I was gay.

Guzim proffered a grovelling apology for his ingratitude in selling the shirt I had gifted him, explaining his inexcusable action was prompted by dire necessity. He'd needed the cash for the bus fare back to Albania to meet his new-born son. Handing me a brown paper bag he said he wished to express his remorse by offering me a small token, a gift he had brought back from Albania. Fortunately he kept up a running commentary as I opened the bag; otherwise I may have had difficulty recognising the strange looking contents as a pair of mittens knitted from loose rabbit fur. Not just any random rabbit fur he assured me, but fur from his very own rabbits fashioned into stylish mitts by his wife. I churlishly thought it would take a leap of imagination to describe the bedraggled mittens as stylish, but then again I had no idea what passed as stylish in his part of the world. Guzim urged me to try them on for size; they were a very tight fit and a tad itchy. Naturally the only fitting response was to offer Guzim a bottle of Amstel.

As Guzim guzzled his breakfast beer I clarified that he was free to resume his gardening duties. He told me he would start work that very afternoon, preparing the vegetable patch as we'd need to get started planting potatoes, onions, broccoli and cauliflower. He didn't seem too thrilled when I told him that Nikos was looking for someone to help out with the olive harvest, muttering under his breath that Nikos was a slave driver who only paid a pittance. I'd already worked that out for myself. Nevertheless I leapt to Nikos' defence, saying he was getting on in years and needed the help of a strong young man, especially as Dina was incapacitated. Guzim said he would think about it, nonchalantly lobbing the empty beer bottle into my garden before going on his way.

No sooner had Guzim departed than Barry appeared, rubbing his forehead where he'd just been hit with the flying beer bottle.

"I've been lurking in the undergrowth waiting for Guzim to leave, I didn't want him gossiping that I'd stayed out all night, Cynthia has her reputation to consider," Barry explained. "What on earth is that rash on your hands Victor? It looks rather painful."

"It appears as though I have contracted a fungal skin infection from contaminated rabbit fur," I said, staring in horror at my red and itchy hands.

"But you don't have any rabbits," Barry pointed out.

"No indeed, but it appears Guzim's rabbits are infected with dermatophytosis and I have contracted it through sticking my hands in these contaminated mittens. I must buy some anti-fungal cream the moment the pharmacy opens."

"You'd best hide your hands away in a pair of Marigold's Marigolds. She'll have a fit if she sees you've turned scaly before her big dinner party," Barry quipped, craftily sneaking by me to claim first dibs on the hot water.

Chapter 16

A Perfect December Day

The early December sunshine streaming into the house cast light into every corner, lifting my mood. Our traditional Greek house already had a homely feel even though it was relatively new to us. I opened the French windows to step outside onto the balcony, inhaling a deep breath of fresh mountain air, scented with pine, citrus and a hint of olive wood smoke. Fallen leaves from the plane trees shading the village square rustled on the street below, a sign that autumn seemed to put in a later appearance than it did back in England. It was hard to imagine that by late afternoon the temperature would drop dramatically and a fire would be needed to warm the house in the evening. The two mutant kittens followed me outside, one possessively claiming its place on a chair, stretching out in the sunshine with its belly exposed in hope of a tickle, the other making an optimistic leap from the balcony, its fall fortunately cushioned by the carpet of red and gold leaves below.

"I've a feeling that one is going to need all of its nine lives," Marigold said, joining me on the balcony. "He's a real dare devil."

"He takes after his father," I said, wondering if the infamous Kouneli had perhaps been crossbred with a rabbit since the kitten had a decided look of a mutant buck bunny about him. Our two imported cats, being spoilt domestics, rarely ventured outdoors, but Clawsome's offspring didn't share her inhibitions.

"I'm so happy the weather has cleared up in time for Geraldine's visit, it's her first ever trip to Greece you know," Marigold said. Geraldine had already phoned to let us know that her plane had touched down safely in Athens and she had booked a seat on the early morning bus through to town, where we would collect her at noon.

"Don't forget to throw the beach bag in the car Victor, Geraldine may want to stop for a swim on the coast, I've already got my costume on under my sun dress. Imagine the delight of a dip on a day like this."

Marigold's choice of clothes would make us stand out like a couple of tourists rather than seasoned Europeans who'd made our home in Greece. Even though the day was marked by glorious sunshine I knew that the local Greeks would be suitably attired for winter, wrapped up in thick flannel shirts, scarves and boots. Many of the local men were already sporting the unshaven look, telling me a winter beard and an early morning raki helped them to stave off the early morning cold when they worked out-doors.

Marigold's cheery mood was infectious and I reflected that one of the benefits of moving to Greece was the chance to be more spontaneous and give in to the impulse for a sudden dip. We had often driven over to Southport from Man-chester on clear winter weekend days. Marigold had enjoyed treating my credit card to an outing in the up-market Wayfarers Arcade, a boulevard of

Victorian fronted shops under a famed glass dome, before we shared a bracing walk across the sand dunes. We had never been tempted to strip down and swim in the Irish Sea though. Here in Greece we were afforded a certain anonymity down on the coast that we didn't enjoy in the village. If the villagers were to spot us plunging into, what was to us, still unseasonably warm water, they would consider such rash behaviour the height of folly, akin to our view of anyone braving the Irish Sea in December.

I had heard many opinionated views from the local villagers that only madmen and tourists were foolish enough to bathe out of season; they would never be reckless enough to risk pneumonia by shedding their warm layers at this time of year. I had noticed a tendency for the Greeks to refer to swimming as bathing, initially finding this turn of speech rather confusing. When they declared that they didn't take a *banyo* in winter I had jumped to the erroneous conclusion that they objected to taking baths during the coldest months of the year, a most unhygienic practice. Fortunately Spiros cleared up my misunderstanding by explaining the word *banyo* covered a multitude of things from bathroom, shower and bath, to swimming;

though I did wonder if Guzim's hosepipe would see much action once the sunshine disappeared.

"It's certainly a beautiful day for our drive up to town," I agreed. "If Geraldine isn't too exhausted from her journey, a swim sounds most agreeable."

"Have you decided on a menu for tomorrow evening's dinner party?" Marigold asked.

"I think I'll prepare something typically Greek," I replied. "After Nikos' reluctance to taste my mulled wine I have reached the obvious conclusion that the local Greek palate isn't very adventurous."

"Nonsense Victor, I'm sure our guests would appreciate something different as a nice change from their usual Greek fare. I'm quite in the mood for a curry and some of our guests may have never tried it before."

"That's what I'm afraid of," I admitted.

"You can be such a worrywart Victor, there was nothing at all Greek about my sherry trifle yet the bowl was practically licked clean. It just shows our guests will be open to trying new cuisines."

"Well Spiros certainly enjoyed your trifle," I agreed, recalling how Spiros was a bit of a maverick, flouting the local Greek custom of not eating basil. I considered perhaps Panos and Dimitris would prove to be equally receptive, but somehow doubted it. The older clientele at the taverna were very set in their ways, expecting bread, cheese, Greek salad and grilled meat with chips every night. There was never any variation in Nikos' food; though rumour had it that he often got Dina to deep fry dried *bakaliaros* during the winter. Perhaps he didn't trust my fish frying capabilities as yet.

The locals were very vocal in their revulsion of Barry's habit of drowning his chips in vinegar, shaking their heads in wonder at this bizarre foreign practice and questioning why he didn't just squeeze a lemon over his potatoes. Personally I liked the Greek habit of squeezing lemon over grilled meat and sprinkling fresh oregano on top of everything, finding both additions enhanced the natural flavours. I had gathered from our conversations that the typical Greek lunch consisted of yet more bread and salad, served with a traditional dish such as *moussaka, keftedes* meatballs, or *fasolada* authentic bean soup, reinforcing my belief that my new friends would not be particularly open to sampling foreign food.

"I'm sure Geraldine would appreciate a

traditional Greek meal," I suggested.

"Geraldine's taste buds have been completely ruined by taste testing pet food," Marigold countered. "I'm lucky I escaped the same fate. She does enjoy a curry though; her palate is quite immune to the spices."

Admitting defeat I agreed to create an Indian feast for our dinner party, thinking I might serve onion bhajis, followed by a mild chicken tikka masala prepared in the slow cooker. If I served it with a piquant Indian cucumber salad and naan bread our Greek guests would at least have the requisite salad and bread on the table to meet their expectations.

Our drive up to the bus station to meet Geraldine was a sheer pleasure. The sky was clear and blue, the temperature just perfect, lacking the cloying humidity of summer. I drove slowly to appreciate the sight of the local villages beginning their preparations for the olive harvest. Many of the olive groves we drove past were blanketed with heavy old black tarpaulins, the more traditional style of olive net in the area, interspersed with flashes of the more modern green olive nets. As we began to drive up the mountain the olives groves transformed from flat fields into steep terraces. I imagined they must present a challenge to the olive farmers attempting to balance their three-legged ladders on angled surfaces. Donkeys seemingly had right of the way on the road, laden with olive tree branches and led by elderly gents wrapped up in enough layers to withstand a sudden hurricane. As we climbed the mountain we looked down on the sea, calm, blue and inviting, reaffirming our decision to stop off for a swim later.

"If the weather remains as perfect as this we'll be able to enjoy a few day trips out with Geraldine. When you think about it, winter in Greece is the ideal time for a holiday, it isn't too hot to walk about and take in the sights," Marigold enthused. "A trip out to a few ruins may put things into perspective for Geraldine and make her realise she isn't past it yet."

"Of course she isn't past it, she's what, a good five years younger than you?"

"Yes, but she feels she's wasted so much time dating the wrong men that time is slipping by. I know how you make fun of her seeming desperation to get married but she only wants someone to come home to at the end of the day. It can't be much fun planning holidays alone and heating up ready meals for one."

"I feel a tad guilty that Barry and I have

judged Geraldine's desire to meet someone and get married as a sign of spinster desperation," I said apologetically, thinking it had been unkind to malign her as a man-mad harpy. "I suppose it is only natural that she wants to meet a loving partner rather than the inevitable losers she wastes her time on. After all she has our example of the perfect marriage to emulate."

"Oh for goodness sake Victor, have you any idea how pompous you sound," Marigold chided. "Is it any wonder that I often envy Geraldine's single state?"

As the car rounded a sharp bend I slammed my foot on the brake to avoid running over an elderly lady dressed in traditional black widow weeds. She was risking life and limb by standing in the middle of the road waving her walking stick.

"What are you doing Victor?" Marigold asked.

"She may need assistance, she appears to be in distress," I replied, waiting for the elderly lady to hobble over to the car. Smiling widely the lady named a village situated off a side road, perhaps eight kilometres along the road we were travelling. We hadn't yet explored the many villages sited above the road, though they were on our to-do bucket list. As we drove right by the turning to the village she mentioned I was happy to offer her a lift, thinking she made an unusual hitchhiker. Thanking me profusely for my kindness she doddered over to the side of the road to collect two bulging carrier bags before struggling into the back seat, apologising as her walking stick clipped me soundly on the ear.

Delighted by this unexpected opportunity to practice my Greek I asked her if she'd been shopping, a natural conversation starter considering her two bulging carrier bags. Unfortunately she couldn't make head or tail of what I was asking, despite my repeating the question four times. My skill in the language was hampered by my inability to correctly pronounce the Greek word for shopping; it proved impossible to get my tongue around the 'ps' combination that *'psonisie'*, the word for shopping, required. I had encountered the same challenge when attempting to say bread and fish in Greek, but it was much easier to make a stab at the strange pronunciation when looking someone directly in the face. In this instance our elderly hitchhiker could only converse with the back of my head.

Changing my tack I asked if she had been to the shops. Thrilled to be able to understand me she began to chat ten to the dozen. Able to pick out about one word in three, I think she told me she had been to visit her sister and her bags were full of fresh produce from the garden. Next we moved onto the weather, agreeing it was a beautiful day. Thinking I was on a roll I was happy to answer her questions about the number of children we had, telling her we just had one son who was thirty-five. Marigold was in her element when I translated that our hitch-hiker said that she didn't look old enough to have a grown man as a son. I fell into a sticky wicket when our hitch-hiker asked about Benjamin's wife and children, not sure if it would offend the sensibilities of an aged Greek pensioner if I tried to explain our son was out and proud.

We had reached the turn off to the village our elderly hitch-hiker had mentioned, the signpost indicating it was four kilometres up the side of the mountain. It seemed very rude to just dump her at the side of the road; it was really quite hot and she may not be able to hitch another lift for hours, so I made the decision to take the turning to her village. I had no problem translating her gushing *"ena toso kalo agori,"* since I was used to hearing Dina saying the exact same thing when she told me I was such a good boy for helping. The woman's gratitude was palpable but I brushed off her excessive thanks with a casual *tipota*, saying it was nothing. She tapped me on the shoulder, nearly knocking my ear off with her walking stick, to indicate I should stop outside a small house on the side of the road leading into the village. Telling me it was her house, she invited us inside for coffee and fruit. She seemed genuinely disappointed when I said we didn't have time, we had to meet a bus at the bus station. Hating to see her struggle with two heavy bags and a walking stick, I carried her bags to the door, once again refusing her offer of coffee due to time constraints. Telling me to wait one minute she disappeared inside, returning to press a jar of home produced olives on me before waving us away.

Marigold and I both agreed it had been a pleasant encounter, though Marigold asserted she really needed to make more effort to master the Greek language. She'd been a bit lax about keeping her attendance up at Greek classes, whilst my evenings working in the taverna had improved my own skills immensely. I certainly had a long way to go in mastering the language, but at least I could converse with random old ladies picked up on a mountain, as long as I steered away from the unpronounceable subject of shopping.

Sunday turned out to be the perfect day to drive into town. All the shops were closed, thus sparing my credit card from one of Marigold's spending sprees. Traffic was much quieter too. Usually the approach to the bus station was quite fraught, horns blasting from bumper to bumper cars, drivers and motorcyclists weaving erratically between lanes and double parking. The approach was clear and we were able to easily park on the side of the road. The bus from Athens hadn't arrived yet so we took a seat in a simple cafe opposite the bus station, sipping on cold glasses of pear juice and enjoying a spot of people watching whilst we waited for Geraldine to arrive.

Chapter 17

A Winter Banyo

When the bus pulled in I felt a slight sinking feeling, knowing that my regular routine would be disrupted by the presence of an unwanted house guest. I was used to Barry being around. He was so familiar he was practically part of the furniture, but other house guests tended to be more disruptive, expecting entertaining conversation and to be waited on hand and foot. Nevertheless I decided to put a brave face on for Marigold's sake, reminding myself it was only for a week.

Geraldine was perfectly pleasant, just a tad obsessed with bagging herself a husband even though her potential victims tended to be highly unsuitable marriage material.

Geraldine blended in quite well with the Greek ladies stepping down from the bus, dressed for travelling in warm winter clothes. As she and Marigold embraced in greeting, I made a grab for her suitcase as it emerged from the bowels of the bus.

"I can't believe how hot it is," Geraldine enthused. "It was miserable, damp and cold when I flew out of Manchester. I'm completely overdressed for this lovely weather."

"Why not grab a change of outfit from your suitcase and slip it on in the ladies' room? We were going to suggest a swim on the way home if you aren't too jet lagged," Marigold suggested, ignoring the fact that our guest hadn't flown transatlantic.

"Oh that sounds fabulous," Geraldine trilled. "I was a bit tired when the plane landed, but this wonderful Greek air has quite revived me. Would you mind if we found somewhere else for me to change though? I'd like to get out of the bus station quickly in case this awful old harridan who has stalked my every step from

Manchester airport puts in an appearance."

"Of course," Marigold agreed. "We'll stop at a nice sea front hotel for a coffee and a bite of lunch, you can use their facilities to slip into your costume. It's awful when you get stuck with someone ghastly on an aeroplane and there's nowhere to escape. Imagine being saddled with someone like Harold on a four hour flight, Victor, it would be enough to make one want to bolt through the nearest emergency exit."

Cringing at the very thought of being stuck on a flight with Harold, I felt a twinge of sympathy for Geraldine. As someone who made an effort to get along with everyone, she must have had to endure someone quite frightful on the flight if it led her to complain so vociferously.

"It wasn't just the flight; I was stuck with her on the bus ride too, all the way from Athens. I hate to sound like a snob, but she was dreadfully common and very loud. I'd planned to sleep on the flight over but it was quite impossible with this awful old woman in the seat behind me complaining about everything at full volume. I couldn't believe my bad luck when she was on the same bus from Athens. She seemed quite oblivious to the very strange looks she was receiving from the other passengers, she must have the hide of a rhino."

"Don't worry; you aren't likely to run into her again, most English people stay down on the coast. We don't tend to get tourists up in our village because it's a bit off the beaten track," I assured Geraldine, carrying her suitcase to the car. "Mind you, we don't tend to get many tourists at all out of season."

"Thank goodness you are staying with us. Imagine if you had to put up with that sort of person staying in the same hotel," Marigold said.

"It doesn't bear thinking about," Geraldine shuddered. "At least some poor sap will be spared from having her put a damper on their hotel break since she made it known she's staying with family in Greece."

"I wonder if Harold has his mother visiting," Marigold speculated with a laugh.

"Oh don't," I said, trying to imagine what sort of vile creature must have spawned Harold, though I'd hazard a guess she fitted Geraldine's description of loud and vulgar.

We decided to stop at a seafront hotel for coffee and then take a dip in the sea there since Geraldine was itching to get in the water, before ordering lunch. It was the first time we'd stopped on this stretch of beach out of season. The vast stretch of sand disappeared into the horizon, looking so different without its regimented layers of sunbeds and umbrellas. There was hardly a soul in the water and the beach was equally deserted.

"I can't believe we have this paradise all to ourselves," Geraldine exclaimed. "You really have done well for yourselves moving over here. The views from the bus were quite captivating, but this is absolutely breath-taking."

"I'm afraid we can't offer you a beach up in Meli, but we do have stunning views of the sea," I said, feeling immensely grateful that Vangelis had fixed the loose plank in the fence surrounding Guzim's shed. I wasn't too sure how Geraldine may have reacted to the spare bedroom view of the Albanian showering under the hosepipe.

"It sounds heavenly," Geraldine said, wincing at her first sip of strong Greek coffee. "This is going to be just the relaxing break I need to get over that humiliating break-up; it was so terribly crass of him to dump me by email."

"So crass and insensitive," Marigold agreed.

"Well I have to say I didn't think much of

him from the off, he liked the sound of his own voice way too much," I said, recalling the extremely tedious supermarket auditor who had bored us all silly with the intimate details of his desperately dull stocktaking duties at Tesco when we'd all met up for dinner in the summer.

"But you never met him Victor," Geraldine said.

"Of course I did, remember we all had dinner together in Chinatown. He was clueless how to manage his chopsticks and he droned on all evening about bar codes. He had no idea how boring he was," I argued.

"You're confusing William with Tim, William was the auditor who broke up with Geraldine back in August because he was scared of commitment, still at least he had the decency to tell her to her face," Marigold said.

"It was a bare faced lie though," Geraldine interjected. "Three weeks later he announced his engagement to a check out assistant."

"Oh I know, you think he'd have been a bit more discreet about it to spare your feelings. Victor, we never met Tim, we'd already moved over here when Geraldine started seeing him. I must have told you all this a hundred times Victor, do you never listen to a word I say?"

Marigold said with a withering look.

"Of course I do dear, but I can't be expected to keep up with every convoluted detail of Geraldine's love life, she has a new boyfriend every other month," I snapped. Catching sight of Geraldine's look of embarrassment I hastened to add, "No offence Geraldine, I'm sure it can't be easy finding someone suitable at your age, I wouldn't know where to start dating, though I gather from Barry that the lonely hearts columns are best avoided, full of desperate stalkers apparently."

"Well I did try hanging round in the bucket aisle of B & Q but it didn't bring me any luck," Geraldine quipped with a knowing wink. "Anyway, as Marigold said, you never actually met Tim; in fact he seemed reluctant to meet any of my friends."

"Do you suppose he was secretly married?" Marigold suggested, a look of outraged horror contorting her features.

"Oh no, he was definitely single, he just had an aversion to any sort of activity that might involve spending money. He liked to come over for a home cooked meal in the evenings because it was a bit tricky cooking in his bed sit, Tim said it tended to trigger the smoke alarms,"

Geraldine explained. He sounded like a free-loader to me, but I decided to keep my own counsel.

"The email came after I suggested we take a mini-break together. He accused me of being a shallow spendthrift when I said a night in his tent at Hollingsworth Lake wasn't quite what I had in mind. I wasn't expecting the Ritz but really, a tent in December; it's been raining so much lately we'd probably have been washed into the dratted lake."

"He sounds like a miserly skinflint, you're obviously better off without him," Marigold commiserated.

"On the bright side I'd already booked the time off work for the mini-break that never transpired, so I was free to get a last minute flight over here," Geraldine said. "But Marigold you're right about me being better off without Tim. I always seem to end up putting up with boring types like William or totally unsuitable skinflints like Tim, just so I can be part of a couple. That's why I've decided not to meet any more new men for the foreseeable."

"A very wise decision," I concurred.

"Now don't be too hasty Geraldine, we all have to kiss a few frogs before we find our prince," Marigold said. "Best to get straight back on the horse I think."

"I'm sure Geraldine knows her own mind," I argued, wondering why my wife was so intent on interfering and just how many frogs she'd kissed before we fortuitously met.

"She will just have to change her mind back again then since we have three eligible bachelors expected for dinner tomorrow evening," Marigold reminded me, seemingly forgetting Geraldine was there.

Geraldine immediately perked up at this news, admitting, "I'm sure it won't do any harm to meet them. It's very kind of you to arrange it Marigold."

"Well I'll be the one toiling over a hot stove all day," I interjected.

"Oh don't exaggerate Victor; all you have to do is throw a curry in the slow cooker. Now, who's ready for that swim, the water does look inviting?"

Geraldine excused herself to change into the bikini she had retrieved from her suitcase. I took the opportunity to remind my wife that she still had to break the news to Geraldine that we had a houseful of cats, no small thing considering our houseguest suffered from ailurophobia.

BUCKET TO GREECE (VOL. 2)

"It's one thing to have an irrational fear of cats in the abstract Victor, it's quite another matter to resist the charms of Clawsome, Catastrophe and the adorable kittens," Marigold said, blithely dismissing Geraldine's phobia. "Anyway I've kept the cats out of the best guest bedroom since Barry pretended to move into your office. If Geraldine really doesn't take to them we can shut them up in your office."

I made a mental note to stash the newly penned first chapters of my book in a secure box to be placed out of reach of the kittens. After suffering the tragic loss of my first masterpiece to the shredder I had no wish to see my second attempt used as cat litter.

The sea was a tad chilly, or should I say invigorating, but very relaxing once we got used to the buoyancy of the gentle waves. I reflected that Manchester may be investing millions of pounds in its flashy new aquatic centre but I was sure it couldn't rival the wonderful experience of swimming in the sea in December with the brooding majesty of Taygetos as a backdrop. I decided that I would be proud to announce to the taverna regulars that I was one of the mad foreigners prepared to risk a *banyo* in winter. I took advantage of the opportunity to improve my butterfly stroke whilst the ladies' bobbed and chatted. Working in the taverna kitchen would play havoc with my trim physique if I didn't make some effort to exercise since I liked to taste test the chips for quality before sending them out to the customers.

After our dip we dried off in the sunshine over a pleasant lunch of Greek salad and fried *kalamari*. The handsome waiter turning on the typical Greek charisma for the ladies made me reflect that I was a lucky man indeed to be in such charming company. Marigold looked attractively elegant with her silk wrap modestly draped over her swimming costume, her damp red locks reflecting the sunlight. Geraldine's joy at being on vacation in the sunshine transformed her average features and I suspected she may well tickle Spiros' fancy. Considering her appalling lack of judgement when it came to men, she wasn't likely to be off-put by his profession of undertaker. He could certainly make his corpses sound more exciting than a Tesco stocktake audit.

Marigold and Geraldine enjoyed a glass of wine, but as the permanently designated driver

BUCKET TO GREECE (VOL. 2)

I stuck to sparkling water, not wishing to end up in a ditch like Harold. I decided it really was high time Marigold got to grips with the left-hand drive Punto. My reasoning was not entirely selfish; she would be able to venture beyond the village with Geraldine whilst I was working in the evenings and the longer she procrastinated the more difficult she would find it. We never knew when she might be required to drive in an emergency.

The drive back to Meli was a pleasurable experience since Geraldine's enthusiastic running commentary on every, to her, novel aspect of the journey, was oddly contagious. Of course we hadn't lived in the area for long enough to become jaded or take the breath-taking magnificence of the scenery for granted, but it seemed as though we were seeing it all for the first time through Geraldine's eager eyes as she oohed over the stunning views and aahed at the hairpin bends, exclaiming at the by now familiar goats bringing the traffic to a halt as they gambolled leisurely across the road.

"It's like stepping back in time," Geraldine said as I slowed down to give a laden down donkey right of way, "and such friendly people," she added when the old man leading the donkey returned her cheery wave.

"We have found the Greek people to be very accepting and friendly," I said, thinking of the new friendships I was developing.

I was gratified to notice that Marigold had promoted me from kitchen skivvy when she asked Geraldine, "Did Victor mention that he's got an evening job as a chef in the local taverna?"

"I'm just helping out until the owner's wife recovers the use of her broken arm," I clarified modestly.

"Still, fancy that. I remember the days when Victor's culinary talents only extended to heating up Fray Bentos pies in a tin," Geraldine giggled.

"He still has a weakness for them," Marigold confessed, most likely pre-empting any sarcastic remarks if Geraldine were to discover my secret stash in the kitchen. "He quite enjoys experimenting in the kitchen these days and of course when he's in charge of the cooking I don't have him stood over my shoulder, spraying every surface with sanitiser."

"You can never be too careful when it comes

to lurking bacterial microbiologicals and micro-bials," I reminded Marigold.

"I was watching 'Frasier' last week Victor and I have to say he reminded me of you," Geraldine said.

"No doubt his debonair style and erudite ways struck a chord," I preened, quite liking the comparison to the suave character cast in the role of radio psychiatrist.

"No, it was his obsession with wringing out the kitchen sponge to prevent bacteria breeding on it that reminded me of you," Geraldine clarified.

Geraldine's anticipation grew when we told her we were on the final approach to Meli, eager to see the village we had made our new home. As we drove into the village it was reminiscent of our first visit there when Spiros drove us up for the house viewing.

"Away from the maddening crowd of tourists you will breathe pure mountain air in peace and tranquillity," I said, paraphrasing the words Spiros had uttered on that memorable occasion.

"There are no crowds of maddening tourists Victor, it is December," Marigold interjected, ruining the poetry of the moment.

Chapter 18

Sweet Chestnuts

Geraldine's reaction to our home in Meli was as enthusiastic as her reaction to everything else she had thus far encountered in Greece. She admired the flowering plants in earthenware pots lining the outdoor staircase leading up the front door, and raved over the interior of the house. She was particularly impressed when Marigold whipped out the before and after photographs to illustrate the work we'd had done, praising Marigold's vision in spotting the potential of the dated house we'd purchased, its finer points hidden away below endless clutter, layers of greasy linoleum and cheap chip board. She was enthralled by the stunning views from the roof terrace, reminding me how Marigold had fallen for the house from this vantage point before even stepping inside, seduced by the rolling vista.

Barry put in a polite appearance, greeting Geraldine cordially. He made it clear right off the bat that he was spoken for by saying he would be spending the evening with Cynthia. Geraldine thanked him profusely for giving up the best spare bedroom for her, a room Marigold had transformed into an oasis of calm. She was obviously curious why he didn't just simply stay over at Cynthia's place rather than move his things into my office and sleep on the sofa-bed.

I was gob-smacked when Geraldine rushed over to scoop up the mutant kittens, burying her face in their fur and exclaiming they were simply adorable. It appeared Marigold had rather exaggerated her friend's irrational fear of cats, unless she had mistaken them for deviant rabbits. I fired a withering look in Marigold's direction when Geraldine proclaimed the sweet little things could sleep on her bed; it had been pointless to bother changing the sheets, Geraldine would clearly have no objection to sleeping on a bed of cat hair.

"I was under the impression you suffered from virulent ailurophobia," I said, somewhat relieved that at least we wouldn't be forced to lock the cats away in my office.

"Oh no, I adore cats, the phobia was just a convenient excuse I concocted at work to get moved from taste testing cat food to a new line of luxury bird seed we were trialling. I was piling on the pounds with the cat food line and thought bird seed would be better for my figure. You don't find such tasty additions as sultanas and juniper berries in cat food," Geraldine confessed breezily.

"I remember now," Marigold said. "You were so convincing I'd completely forgotten your cat phobia was fabricated."

Deciding I would leave the girls alone to enjoy a gossipy catch-up, I excused myself, saying I wanted to call in on Dimitris before heading to the taverna to peel the potatoes for that evening's chips. Marigold reminded me not to accept any excuses from Dimitris: she was expecting him to play his part as an eligible bachelor the next evening. Geraldine said the travelling on top of the time difference was beginning to catch up with her. The two women were happy to spend a quiet night in by the fire as Geraldine needed an early night. Marigold said she'd see me in the morning, reminding me not to forget to leave my clothes on the balcony if I came home smelling like a chip shop.

I was just about to leave when Dina arrived bearing a gift of homemade *kastana glykisma*, sweet spoon chestnuts, to welcome our guest. I was touched by her kind gesture, telling her she shouldn't have gone to so much trouble, knowing it must have been very difficult to peel chestnuts with only one arm. I was amazed and delighted when Dina told me that Nikos had taken charge of the peeling; I would use this precious information to mercilessly rib him later about doing 'the woman's work'. Geraldine enthused over the sticky spoon sweets, a culinary novelty to her. I explained that Dina had prepared the chestnuts by cooking them in a mixture of sugar, honey and cinnamon.

I was obliged to delay my departure to prepare unnaturally sweet coffee for Dina, Marigold's Greek not yet being proficient enough to leave her comfortably alone with the older woman. Geraldine was suitably impressed with my burgeoning language skills, oblivious that my tenses were inaccurate and I was continually dropping embarrassing malapropisms which Dina kindly overlooked.

Sampling the delicious sweet chestnuts reminded me of an outing Marigold and I had enjoyed back in October when we'd driven to one of the nearby mountain villages to celebrate their annual chestnut festival. The village square had been filled with the tantalizing aroma of roasted chestnuts and it had been fascinating to watch the villagers stir a vast vat of boiling chestnuts. We had wandered around makeshift stalls selling quince and chestnut spoon sweets, mountain herbs, walnuts, and locally made tsipouro renowned for its potency. As the day progressed the familiar strains of Greek dance music filled the air and locals appeared in traditional Greek costumes, encouraging the visitors to spontaneously join the Greek dancers.

My attempts to master the *sirtaki* unfortunately confirmed Marigold's long held accusations that I had two left feet. My wife appeared to have a natural bent for the dance steps, proclaiming we must sign up for classes. Fortunately my two left feet convinced her she would progress more speedily in the art of Greek dance if she found a girl friend to go along with her instead of me.

I was able to translate Dina's recollections that during the war chestnuts had been a vital form of sustenance, ground down into bread. I was always intrigued to hear snippets of the older villagers' memories of times past, fascinated to think how different their lives must have been before the advent of electricity and modern conveniences. Of course Dina hadn't exactly moved with the times, maintaining the centuries old custom of baking bread in an outdoor oven rather than embracing the modern trend of simply throwing a packet of bread mix into an automatic bread maker. It was rare to hear the villagers speak of their experiences during the war or the civil war; Dimitris had explained to me that such talk invariably led to political arguments that inevitably became very heated.

When Dina left I made my way to Dimitris' house, happy to find him sitting on the doorstep immersed in a book. I felt a tad guilty that he felt obliged to accept my dinner invitation for the next evening in gratitude for my role of phone a friend on Millionaire. Dinner parties were obviously not his thing. I decided it would be tactful to not mention his presence was required to make up the numbers of eligible bachelors my wife intended to dangle like juice morsels in front of her best friend.

Dimitris confided he had hated every moment of being under the cameras. He had considered the whole process demeaning, making a spectacle of himself for money, amazed by the banality of the questions.

"I expected the questions to be the serious ones about philosophy, history, poetry, religion and science. I should have to known when Spiros offered to be the phone friend for the movies that the show covered frivolities."

"Do you mean to say you'd never actually seen the television show before you appeared on it?" I asked.

"Spiros explained the little about it and I planned to watch it before I went to Athens, but the theme music brought me out in the sweat," Dimitris confessed, reminding me how much he'd publicly perspired on camera. "Still it was the worth it to win the five thousand euros, it is the lot of money. I must to share it with you Victor to repay your help."

"There's absolutely no need for that," I assured him. "It was reward enough to be able to help you. Nikos was so impressed by my knowledge of the Asia 1 virus that led to the small outbreak of foot and mouth disease in Greece in 2000 that he finally listened to my concerns about feeding swill to his pigs and has promised to put an end to the vile practice."

"You mean I cannot to feed any leftovers to my pig?" Dimitris said.

"I didn't even know you kept a pig," I replied.

"I buy one with my winnings, the pigs is the intelligent animal and I think it would make the good companion, better than the woman," Dimitris said with a nervous laugh.

"Well feeding it leftovers is an invitation to disease," I assured him, thinking I'd better not mention to Marigold that Dimitris considered pigs made better companions than women or she would probably insist I disinvite him. Even though he was clearly reluctant to attend it would be rude to rescind the invitation once it had been extended.

"It is good that you have the knowledge to give advice on these things," Dimitris said, sarcastically adding, "Who was to know we Greeks have being doing things the wrong way for years and have been feeding the pigs by the flawed method."

"Swill is just not the best practice. I do speak with a certain authority, being a specialist in food hygiene, and health and safety legislation," I replied huffily.

"And how many the companion pigs you keep in your house in Manchester?" Dimitris snapped, before reddening and apologetically saying, "I did not to mean to disparage your knowledge or question your professional aptitude Victor, as you know my area of the expertise is in history and philosophy, not the animal husbandry."

"Perhaps you can share your knowledge of local history this evening, we have a guest over from England who is sure to be fascinated," I suggested.

"I will be delighted to enlighten them," Dimitris assured me. "It will be the other opportunity to practice my English."

"Another opportunity," I corrected him, hoping he wouldn't attempt to smuggle any leftover curry out to his new companion.

"Indeed, now what say you I bring out the *tavli* and teach you the moves?"

Chapter 19

Geraldine is Surprised by Guzim Showering

The next morning I was up with the lark, watching the sunrise whilst enjoying a steaming cup of coffee on the balcony, mesmerised by the rippling movement of the sea in the distance, a solitary vessel making slow headway towards the horizon. The only sounds breaking through the silence were the gentle tinkling of goat bells and the intermittent raucous crows of Nikos' roosters. The day looked promising, the early morning sky hinting we were in for another glorious day of December sunshine. The air was still crisp at this early hour, my favourite time of the day.

As I watched the first signs of village life stirring I made a mental list of the ingredients I would need for the dishes I was planning to cook for that evening's dinner party. The call of the roosters reminded me that Nikos had offered me one of his hens for the curry; I just hoped that he would pluck it before handing it over. I hoped everyone would arrive in a timely fashion for the meal, rather than Greek time; tardiness would mean I wouldn't even get to taste the curry before dashing off to my shift in the taverna. Nikos opened seven evenings a week and as his wife's stand-in I didn't qualify for a day off, though the job did come with the perk of a free hen for the dinner party and as many chips as I could eat.

The early morning peace was disturbed by Geraldine joining me on the balcony, demanding to know if I was aware there was a man clad only in underpants, showering under a hose-pipe in the garden.

"Guzim must have worked the plank loose in the fence again," I exclaimed in annoyance, relieved to hear that he kept his pants on to shower.

"Guzim? Is he one of the eligible bachelors Marigold has invited to dinner?" Geraldine asked in a tone hopeful the illegal Albanian would be making up the numbers. Obviously he'd made an impression, being too far away for her to notice he was practically toothless.

"He hasn't received an invitation," I clarified. Seeing Geraldine's crest fallen expression I hastened to explain that Guzim was a married man with four children and a collection of rabbits infected with dermatophytosis. "He lives in the shed at the bottom of the garden."

"How on earth does he manage to cram a wife, four children and a warren of rabbits into that tiny space?" Geraldine asked.

"He doesn't, he works in Greece to support his family back in Albania," I explained, not mentioning his profligate habit of spending most of his wages on Amstel.

"What a noble sacrifice to be separated from his family," Geraldine gushed.

"Well I do what I can to help, I employ him to help with the garden and only recently I gave him a shirt," I said, loftily drawing attention to my altruistic nature.

I was amazed when Marigold joined us. She

usually avoided getting up at such an early hour, but she obviously felt obliged to put in an appearance due to Geraldine's presence.

"We were just talking about that poor man reduced to living in your shed," Geraldine told her.

"It's not our shed, it's his shed. It is altogether a most bizarre arrangement. Victor paid to have a fence erected round the shed so it wouldn't stand out like an eyesore. Don't tell me he's back to his old trick of turning up on the doorstep to gift us our own fruit in exchange for a handout of beer," Marigold sighed, having a low tolerance for Guzim's living arrangements.

"He hasn't called round this morning, but Geraldine caught an eyeful of him showering under the hosepipe," I explained.

"You must have a word with him Victor; he can't go around flashing his bits in front of our guest," Marigold wailed, clearly affronted by the indignity of the situation.

"Apparently he showers in his underpants," I clarified.

"That's hardly the point Victor," Marigold chided, admittedly relieved he hadn't flashed her best friend.

"All right, I'll have a word with him about

him sneaking through the loose plank in the fence," I agreed, thinking he'd wasted no time at all on his return from Albania in undoing Vangelis' repair work on the fence.

Our conversation was interrupted by Barry trying to discreetly sneak back into the house undetected, having once again spent the night with Cynthia. "It's nice and crisp out there this morning, it's the best time of day for a walk," he said when he realised he'd been spotted.

"Weren't you wearing the same clothes yesterday?" Geraldine asked with a raised eyebrow.

After enjoying a leisurely breakfast I needed to pop out to the village shop to buy the cucumber and tomatoes needed for the Indian salad. I suggested the ladies' accompany me as it would give Geraldine a chance to explore the village. As we strolled towards the village square we ran into the impoverished ex-pat Milton. Marigold had ruled him out as a dinner party guest because he didn't meet her eligible bachelor criteria. He told us they were finding the warm weather just wonderful since it allowed them to spend their days outside rather than huddled over the fire, watching the flames consume their meagre wood supply. His comment reminded me I must ask Guzim to drop the pruning wood round at Milton's to use as kindling.

"The new ball and socket certainly appreciates a break from the damp," Milton said, referring to his new hip replacement. "And it's a treat to be able to pen my book outside. Well best get back to it, it won't write itself. A pleasure to run into you old chap, ladies'," Milton said, doffing his straw hat in a gesture of old world politeness.

"What a talented man he must be to pen a book," Geraldine exclaimed.

"He's writing porn," Marigold told her. The two women immediately dissolved into hysterical laughter like a pair of giddy school girls.

"It's actually erotica," I corrected.

"I hope he keeps his identity quiet, it will be a bit of a passion killer if his readers discover their erotica is written by a geriatric pensioner," Geraldine said. I shared her sentiments, considering it was wise for writers in general to adopt a non de plume if they wished to preserve their anonymity, hence my own decision in adopting the pen name of V.D. Bucket for my literary masterpiece on moving to Greece. Thinking I must carve out a quiet hour in my busy schedule to pen a few more pages I suggested giving Marigold a driving lesson later. The sooner she could take off in the Punto with Geraldine, the sooner I would regain some peace and quiet around the house.

"I'm really not very keen to drive left-hand and I'm a bit nervous at the thought of all the sharp bends, I'd hate to drive over the edge," Marigold prevaricated.

"Oh you simply must drive Marigold," Geraldine interjected. "What if something happened to Victor and you needed to drive in an emergency?"

"Exactly. Getting to grips with the Punto is about more than just taking your turn as the designated driver," I added.

Geraldine chimed in again, helping to make my case by saying, "You don't want to turn into the sort of woman who is dependent on her husband when you've always prided yourself on being so independent."

It seemed that these few words from Geraldine were enough to win Marigold over when she'd held out for months against my apparently unpersuasive arguments. She agreed I could give her a refresher lesson when we returned from our walk.

Geraldine was immediately enchanted by the array of goods on display in the village shop, proclaiming she must purchase some miniature bottles of ouzo to take back as holiday gifts for her co-workers. She insisted on treating our cats to a half-dozen tins of her favourite brand of cat food, amazed it was available in Greece.

My menu for the evening's dinner party ran into a snag when I discovered the village shop didn't stock the gram flour I needed for the onion bhajis and we'd neglected to bring any over from England. Staring at the bags of *alevri* on sale I struggled to determine which of the two varieties, soft or strong, equated to self-raising. Since I'd left the pocket dictionary at home I grabbed a bag of each sort, hoping one of them would add a nice crispy finish to the fried onions. Everything else I needed was available with the exception of limes for the salad, but I could substitute a lemon from the garden. I presumed our guests would not be so au fait with the intricacies of Indian food ingredients and thus unlikely to know if I tampered with traditional recipes, and Geraldine's taste buds were too shot to notice.

Geraldine thought the line-up of table and chairs outside the shop, occupied by elderly *tavli* players idling the morning away, most quaint and inviting, surprised to discover the shop also served coffee. "I wish Tesco had a set-up like this," she gushed, accepting my offer to sit down for a coffee in the shade of the plane trees. I warned her we could be in for a long wait for the coffee to arrive, the woman who ran the shop flitting between serving customers and juggling the *briki*. Catching sight of Spiros' hearse parked on one side of the square Geraldine expressed her hopes that the village hadn't suffered a bereavement.

"That's Spiros' hearse, it's so comfortable. Spiros is the local undertaker and a very dear friend, we'd never have got through all the unfathomable Greek bureaucracy without his help," Marigold trilled. "You'll meet him at dinner this evening, he speaks very good English."

"Is he single," Geraldine panted eagerly.

"He is, but he'd rather not be. Unfortunately some women find his profession off-putting," Marigold confided.

"Oh I feel for him, you can't imagine how many men are put off by the thought of my taste testing pet food for a living, openly cringing as though my job automatically means I have dogs' breath. Do you know I've started to fudge the matter of what I do for a living rather than be the butt of insensitive jokes? If I had a pound for every time I've heard the original line 'that will be why your mane is so glossy' I'd be rich by now," Geraldine said, casually running a hand through her indeed glossy hair. "I've started to tell any interesting prospects that I'm involved with branding pet food, rather than admitting I actually sample it."

"People can be so shallow, taste testing is an honourable career with roots stretching back to ancient times," I said. "Alexander the Great introduced the concept of food tasters, known as *edeatros*, to his court, not only to sample food to detect any poison, but to oversee sumptuous banquets. The use of food testers known as *praegustators* was quite commonplace amongst the highest echelons of Ancient Rome who tended to be a tad paranoid about meeting their end through poison."

"Your head is certainly stuffed with a lot of useless information," Geraldine commented. "Pet food tasters don't commonly taste test for poison, it's a bit less glamorous than that."

"There was nothing at all glamorous about meeting one's end through poison. I was just trying to illustrate the historical roots of taste testing," I said. I had never considered Marigold's career to be anything but worthy, being familiar with the skills required. One couldn't just walk in off the street and land a job by proclaiming an enjoyment of eating dog food; it was a skilled position requiring a degree in food science. Marigold had studied for her degree when Benjamin started school, beginning her career as a product development scientist for a biscuit company. The job as a pet food taster was actually a promotion in terms of pay, with a more than generous holiday allowance. Over the years I grew to appreciate how important her role was in ensuring domestic pets received safe, tasty and nutritious food prepared in hygienic surroundings.

My reflections were interrupted by Marigold announcing, "Don't look now, but here comes Harold."

"Is he one of the eligible bachelors expected this evening?" Geraldine asked eagerly, ignoring Marigold's instruction and swivelling round for a better look, sending a cheery wave in Harold's direction.

"For god's sake don't encourage him, we spent our first month over here avoiding his attempts to befriend us and impress us with his swimming pool," I cautioned.

"He has a swimming pool," Geraldine uttered in surprise, obviously impressed.

"He also has a ghastly wife who is as thick as him," Marigold said, making it clear Harold was not to become an object of Geraldine's interest even if he did boast a pool.

"Oh, he just snubbed us, how very rude," Geraldine exclaimed.

"Thank goodness," Marigold and I parroted in unison.

"At least he appears to be alone, there's no sign of the loud and vulgar woman who stalked Geraldine's journey. What a hoot to think she might have turned out to be Harold's mother," I quipped.

"It was just a long shot, she could have belonged to anyone," Marigold said. "It is hard to assess who may have obnoxious relatives."

"The apple doesn't usually fall far from the tree," Geraldine proclaimed.

Chapter 20

Donated Hens and Eggs

Plucking the feathers from Nikos' hand reared generously donated hen, my thoughts turned wistfully to a pre-plucked plastic wrapped chicken from Tesco. Handling a neat little bag of giblets stuffed into a Tesco bird was infinitely preferable to donning a pair of yellow Marigolds to deal with viscous entrails. Luckily the bird looked plump enough to stretch to eight portions of curry, instead of the original six. I had carefully curated a menu for six people; myself, Marigold and

Geraldine, plus the three eligible bachelors Spiros, Dimitris and Panos. Barry had no interest in attending the small soiree until Cynthia got wind of it; offended that she hadn't been invited she made a song and dance about being accustomed to being excluded as a single woman, yet here was the perfect opportunity to attend a dinner party as part of a couple before Barry returned to England.

Naturally Marigold caved in to her brother's request, insisting the two of them must join us, even though we patently only had six dining chairs. I would have to resort to seating two guests in the plastic chairs retrieved from the bins, currently adorning the roof terrace. Whoever landed up in the plastic seats would have to sit on bolster cushions since the plastic ones were a good six inches shorter than the rest of the chairs.

Once the chicken was chopped up and thrown in the slow cooker with the requisite curry spices I prepared the naan bread and coated the sliced onions in batter made from the suspect flour. I was quite enjoying this time alone, appreciating having the house to myself, the poignant notes of Puccini's La Boheme flooding the kitchen without Marigold sniping about the volume of what she described as my 'pretentious music'.

Marigold had adapted very quickly to handling the left-hand drive Punto after a quick practice lesson, easily getting to grips with the gear stick being situated to her right. Always a capable driver, her reluctance to take the wheel had surprised me. It was true that the hair-pin bends could be a tad daunting and the narrow mountain roads a bit of a challenge, but overall I found it much more pleasant to drive over here than suffer the Manchester traffic jams. Marigold confided that the sight of random squashed cats littering the roads made her naturally fearful of driving into a cat, tortoise or fox, since they seemed to lack any road sense. She generously admitted she would rather I was the one responsible for any accidental road-kill in my role as the permanently designated driver.

Once I finally got Marigold to take the wheel she soon felt confident enough to announce she would drive Geraldine down to the coast for lunch and a quick dip. They had to be back by mid-afternoon as Athena had managed to squeeze them into her kitchen for hair appointments so they would look their best for the dinner party. Marigold had taken the precaution of borrowing my pocket English to Greek dictionary to avoid any hairdressing mishaps, proclaiming, "I don't want to accidentally end up with a shaggy perm due to any language misunderstandings."

With the curry cooking away in the slow cooker I treated myself to a simple lunch of soft boiled eggs and soldiers. Litsa's brother, the notorious garlic eater, had pressed a dozen new laid eggs on me in the taverna the previous evening; such largesse counted as tips in the local establishment since the Greeks seemed disinclined to part with their loose change. Naturally there was no comparison between newly laid eggs with their deep yellow yolks and the battery offerings we were used to from Tesco. The soldiers were sliced from the homemade bread I'd had a hand in making; Dina's bread crisped up beautifully and was perfect for dipping.

After lunch I retired to the balcony with my notepad to pen a chapter of my moving abroad book, deciding to include my reasoning for publishing the literary masterpiece under the pseudonym of V.D. Bucket. It proved quite a challenge conjuring up alternate names for my

Greek neighbours to preserve their anonymity. The ringing of the telephone disturbed me, making me realise I'd been lost in thought for the last thirty minutes. It was Marigold calling from Athena's kitchen to inform me she had just invited Vangelis and Athena to attend our dinner party. Athena had been keen to know what special occasion prompted the new hair-dos. Marigold naturally felt it would be rude to exclude Athena and Vangelis from our gathering, thus promptly proffered an invitation, carelessly giving no thought to my seating arrangements.

"And just how do you suppose I am meant to stretch a curry originally intended for six people, to ten?" I enquired in annoyance.

"Use your imagination Victor, surely you can bulk it out with a bit more rice and some extra salad," Marigold said impatiently. I'd have liked to see her reaction if I suddenly announced we were four more for dinner than expected if she'd been the one spending the whole day slaving over a hot stove, though I seemed to have been relegated to the role of home chef since the move.

Barry returned from Cynthia's place, a pensive look on his face. I hoped he hadn't popped back for a hot shower since we now had one extra person making demands on the precarious hot water supply. Joining me on the balcony he confided he was loath to return to England.

"It's not the same now you and Marigold aren't just around the corner anymore, and I will really miss Cynthia when I leave," he admitted. "I'm not sure I'm cut out for a long distance relationship."

"Have you considered asking her to move back to England with you?" I asked.

"It's a thought, but she loves it over here, and there is the matter of her cats to consider. I can't see Kouneli adapting to being a tame domestic after having the run of the village out here. I can't get the thought out of my head of relocating to Greece," Barry said.

"But your removal business is back in England," I pointed out.

"Stan would give me a good price for the business, he's itching to take over," Barry said, referring to his second-in-command.

"But have you considered what you would do for work over here, or even where you would live? Cynthia's place is only rented," I pointed out. Barry was only in his early fifties, too early for retirement even if the business netted him a substantial nest egg.

"I've been mulling a few thoughts over. You know how handy I am, I was thinking of asking Vangelis if he fancied expanding the building business by taking me on as a partner."

I had to admit it sounded like a solid move if Vangelis was inclined to expand. There seemed to be more foreigners moving to the area, particularly near to the coast, needing renovation work on their newly acquired properties. Even those investing in new builds always wanted extra features adding. Marigold and I had laughed at the British propensity for encircling olive trees with decorative miniature walls, thinking the trees had managed to exist quite well before this popular ex-pat project was adopted. A building company with two proficient English speakers would likely do very well, particularly if they proved reliable by actually turning up on the promised day.

It still left the small matter of where Barry would live if he followed through on a move. As much as I am fond of my brother-in-law I wasn't sure about the idea of him moving in with us permanently, though Marigold would be over the moon.

"Well it's still early days and maybe a bit pie in the sky, but let's take a look at your downstairs space. It may lend itself well to conversion," Barry blurted out, biting his lip as he waited to see how I would react. Raising a quizzical eyebrow, I said I would definitely give some thought to the matter.

"But let's just keep this between ourselves for the minute Victor, until I can have a quiet word with Vangelis. I'd hate to get Marigold's hopes up, or Cynthia's, if nothing comes of it," Barry wisely added.

I considered Barry's words, realising he had obviously put a lot of thought into the idea of moving to Greece. Knowing how reluctant he was to return to England I decided to toy with him, saying, "I was so impressed with Dina's outside bread oven that I'm contemplating building one in the garden, well more than contemplating actually, I'm going to do it."

"Don't you mean you're going to ask Vangelis to build it?" Barry said.

"No, not at all, I thought I'd give it a whirl myself, it should be an interesting project," I blithely lied, having no intention of attempting to grapple with the complexities of building such a contraption. "I shall place an order for the necessary bricks tomorrow, it can't be that difficult."

"I'm sorry to say Victor but you just don't have the skills, you'll botch it for sure," Barry protested as I waited for him to take the bait. Any moment now I thought.

"I'd better give Stan a call and see if he can manage without me for another week so I can build the outdoor bread oven for you. Marigold would never forgive me if I allowed you to erect some useless monstrosity in her garden."

"Well if you insist," I said, smugly satisfied I had bought Barry another week in Greece to consider his future.

Chapter 21

A Very Precarious Water Supply

Geraldine had pulled out all the stops to catch the eye of one of the three eligible bachelors my wife intended to dangle before her like juicy morsels. She would have looked very presentable in her neatly fitting red dress if it hadn't violently clashed with the sunburn she'd caught after failing to take heed of my sensible advice that sun protection was vital in the December sunshine. Geraldine's glossy hair had been artfully styled to resemble a draped curtain, cleverly concealing the worst of her sunburnt forehead. Fortunately Marigold had lent her some green face powder designed to tone down the redness; the result could perhaps pass as a natural flush resulting from the heat of the spicy curry, as long as she kept her back to the log fire.

Marigold looked quite lovely in a cream outfit that showed off her figure, her Titian hair teased into provocative tendrils by Athena. I was impressed by the salon-like results Athena could achieve in her kitchen. I reflected that at some point in the evening I must raise with Athena the entirely negligent and risky practice of spraying hazardous products in an environment where food was prepared. Surely since Athena had been pensioned off at fifty due to her hazardous occupation of hairdressing and exposure to dangerous chemicals such as polyvinylprrolidone and carboxymethylcelluose, she ought to be more aware that these poisonous chemicals could seep into the food, exposing it to noxious containments. Fortunately the English to Greek noxious chemicals and communicable virus manual I had acquired at outrageous expense revealed the Greek words for these hairspray poisons were almost identical to the familiar English tongue-twisters.

Barry had made an effort to dress smartly, using an iron and spray starch to add what he imagined was a fashionable sharp crease to his jeans. He was in charge of the log fire for the evening, feeding the flames with more wood before heading off to call for Cynthia, having heeded my advice that Cynthia would appreciate the romantic gesture of his walking her to our door.

"Make sure you give the others a knock on your way," Marigold instructed. "Dinner will be ruined if they stick to the vagaries of Greek time. Do remind them that Victor needs to leave at nine for his shift in the taverna."

Each of our Greek guests had complained they weren't used to eating in the middle of the afternoon, commenting we must keep very strange hours in England. Once I had persuasively advised them to think of our dinner as a very late lunch they seemed to come round to my apparently absurd notion of sitting down for a meal at seven o'clock in the evening more readily. Since moving to Meli we had become accustomed to dining much later than we had back in England, though we would need to readapt again in summer when the standard going-out hour fast forwarded to ten instead of nine.

Of course we could always eat dinner down on the coast at seven, but that would make us look like tourists rather than seasoned Europeans in tune with the local culture.

Athena and Vangelis were the first to arrive, the hairdresser clutching a large handbag which she refused to part with. I couldn't be certain since something may have been lost in translation, but my Greek radar picked up on the words she hissed to Vangelis, telling him if the curry was awful as she suspected she would dispose of it in the enormous handbag. Pouring drinks for our guests I double checked my watch. The others were cutting it fine if they expected appetisers, a main course and an offering of Marigold's sherry trifle, her sole contribution to the meal, before I had to leave. I didn't want Dina, whom I had grown inordinately fond of, to risk getting chip fat on her plaster if I was tardy.

Spiros arrived, closely followed by Panos, Dimitris, Barry and Cynthia. Marigold hastily introduced Geraldine to the three single men. Geraldine's attention panned over Dimitris and Panos, dismissing them as unsuitable prospects since they were both seemingly of pensionable age, Dimitris appearing much older than his actual years. Clearly out of his depth he seemed relieved to be overlooked, downing a large glass of ouzo to calm his nerves. Panos stuck out like a sore thumb, having changed into a very dated formal suit he obviously saved for funerals; pairing it with trainers made a mockery of his attempt to look smart. Fortunately Panos took pity on Dimitris and the two of them were soon engrossed in an animated conversation about pig feeding methods.

Geraldine homed in on Spiros, who was naturally quite a catch. In addition to having the reputation as one of the world's best lovers he also had a magnificent physique, at least according to him. I knew he had a weakness for English tourist women. Since it was out of season the pickings were thin and Spiros seemed quite happy to turn his prodigious Greek charm on Geraldine who responded by fluttering her eyelashes and running her fingers seductively through her glossy hair, whilst hanging on his every word.

I steered the three ladies into the normal dining chairs, leaving the gentleman to scrum it out to avoid the short plastic cast-offs that would put them at a height disadvantage. Marigold made me give up my seat to Panos; being quite short and sturdy the low seating arrangement left his forehead at practically the same level as the table; it would have involved some very contorted manoeuvres to get his fork into the curry. A look of panic spread over Dimitris' face when he realised he was being separated from Panos, his erstwhile pig companion, so I negotiated another seating switch to avoid Dimitris sweating into the salad. Finally with everyone placed, able to reach the table and comfortably converse with someone who spoke the same language, I served the Indian salad and the onion bhajis.

The Indian food was, as I'd suspected, a culinary first for our Greek guests; they had never been exposed to an Indian takeaway on every corner or the mixed delights of Manchester's famous Curry Mile. Fortunately this meant they were unable to make comparisons between my attempts to emulate the Indian dishes and the real thing.

Poking around in his salad whilst muttering under his breath that I'd forgotten the cheese, Panos suddenly turned puce, having chomped down on a chilli chopped into the mix. Spotting his strangulated discomfort I jumped to my feet to fetch him a glass of water, only to discover nothing flowed when I turned on the tap. Fiddling with the faucet did nothing to encourage the water to start pouring. Catching Barry's eye I indicated he should join me by the sink.

"There's no water," I hissed, hoping the guests wouldn't overhear.

"I hear it goes off quite frequently, Vangelis tells me the water supply in the village can be quite precarious," Barry said, making no effort to keep his voice down.

"Is the water off again?" Vangelis questioned from the table, blowing my attempt to keep the inconvenient matter hidden from our guests.

"Not to look so the panic Victor, it happens the often. Not to worry, let the wine to flow instead of the water," Spiros piped up, filling the still puce Panos' glass to the brim with white wine.

"But what will we do if anyone requires the lavatory?" I hissed to Barry. Overhearing my aside to Barry, Marigold came up with the bright idea that we could flush the toilet with a bucket of water, completely missing the point that we had no water to fill said bucket.

"And just where do you suppose we draw the water from," I churlishly snapped.

"We could always sneak over to Harold's swimming pool and filch a couple of buckets full to flush the loo," Barry suggested.

"What you need is the back-up tank. Then when there is no water you still have some, unless the *revma* is off too and then the pump not to work," Vangelis advised.

"*Revma*?" Marigold queried.

"The electricity," Vangelis clarified.

"Does the water go off frequently enough to justify the no doubt astronomical expense of a back-up tank?" I asked.

"It's always going off," Cynthia complained. "It's much worse in the summer when the *Dimarcheio* divert the supplies of the mountain villages down to the coast to ensure the holidaymakers have an adequate supply. There is often a general shortage of water, depending on how much rainfall we experience in the winter."

"What choice do we to have? It would to give the *Ellada* a bad name if the tourists have not the water when they come here to spend the money," Spiros explained, adding, "Much the water is the wasted, from how to say in the English, the *solines ekrixis*?"

"The burst pipes," Vangelis translated, adding "They never bother to fix the bursts, the water run like the river."

"I consider it completely irresponsible that people like Harold are allowed to build swimming pools in an area with water shortages," Cynthia said in a disparaging tone.

"I've been trying to persuade Victor we should have a pool put in the garden," Marigold announced, taking me by complete surprise since she hadn't mentioned it for months. She forestalled Cynthia's look of disapproval by insisting she must come over and use it if we ever took the plunge. Attempting to change the subject before Marigold could win support for her extravagant idea from our guests, who would no doubt all be eager to pop round for a dip in her imagined pool, I interjected.

"Harold tops his pool up with mountain spring water from the village taps down on the coast." We had overheard this little gem when Harold had been boasting about his swimming pool to the potential house buyers he had lunched with on the coast. "Apparently it keeps his water bill down."

"That is the disgrace," Spiros shouted. "The spring water is for the drinking, not for the swimming in. Why he not just to fill his stupid pool with sea water if he is the too cheap to pay?"

"It's very frustrating to think Harold has a pool full of water going begging when we don't even have a bucket of the stuff," Marigold sighed. "Victor, see if there are any ice cubes in the freezer, we can defrost them by the fire in case anyone fancies water."

It suddenly occurred to me that my services may not be required in the taverna that evening as it would be against all health and safety regulations for Nikos to serve food without a ready supply of fresh running water. When I voiced this thought Vangelis immediately thwarted my sudden hope of a night off by telling me Nikos had a back-up tank.

"I do you the quote tomorrow Victor, I think you must to have the extra tank."

Our guests had made suitably polite noises about the onion bhajis, attempting to disguise their obvious suspicion of this strange foreign starter, toying with their forks and shuffling the food. When I collected the plates ready for the change of courses I noticed the onion bhajis had been imaginatively hidden beneath scrumpled paper napkins or artfully hidden amongst leftover salad. The English diners had cleared their plates appreciatively, but only Athena from the Greek contingent presented an empty plate, leading me to guess the remnants of her onion bhaji lurked within the cavernous depths of her enormous handbag.

Hoping the second course would be more enthusiastically received I served the chicken curry with a platter of rice and homemade naan bread.

"This is very the good," Spiros praised with obvious insincerity, having merely dipped one prong of his fork tentatively into the hot sauce, surprising me as I'd thought I could rely on him to be more adventurous. "I think it has the interested mix of spices with the chicken, yes?"

"A perfect blend of spices, ginger and garlic," I confirmed.

"I am surprised by your choice of Indian rather than the Greek food Victor, you being such the grecophile. The Greek palate is not accustomed to spices," Dimitris observed, noticeably not touching anything but the bread, his reluctance to speak in company no doubt overcome with the assistance of wine on top of the ouzo.

"I cook Greek food in the taverna every evening," I pointed out, making a mental note to research if chips were invented by the ancient Greeks. "Anyway the main ingredient of this dish is Greek."

"I can't put my finger on anything typically Greek," Cynthia said pensively.

"I know, it's a Greek chicken," Barry correctly guessed.

"It makes my mouth to feel the fire," Vangelis said, obviously trying to divert attention away from his wife who was attempting to discreetly spoon the curry into her ginormous handbag.

Panos surprised me by declaring the curry was very good, "*einai poli kalo*," adding that I must tell Nikos to serve it in the taverna. I decided to pass on that bright idea. If I meddled with Nikos' menu by suggesting the addition of a foreign theme he would likely go off on an outraged diatribe about a certain foreigner with fancy ideas getting above his station as a kitchen skivvy.

Everyone was chatting amicably and getting along. The food was going down, if not exactly well. The guests that weren't too keen on the food attempted to disguise their disgust for my curry by stuffing themselves with the universally liked naan bread. The wine was flowing, except into my glass; I didn't want to risk being drunk in charge of the deep fat fryer later. A sudden sharp rap on the front door disturbed the party. I reluctantly went to answer it, hoping it wasn't a last minute guest Marigold had neglected to mention; we had run out of plastic chairs and there was no way the curry would stretch to eleven unless Athena upended her handbag onto a plate.

Chapter 22

Piccadilly Circus

I opened the front door onto a moonless night blanketed in impenetrable blackness, the stars a distant embellishment. With no sign of anyone on the doorstep I was about to close the door again when I heard the sound of laboured breathing. Peering into the darkness through narrowed eyes I found myself suddenly nose-to-nose with our eighty-year-old next door neighbour, Kyria Maria. Dressed in her customary black widow weeds she was entirely swallowed up in the darkness.

Considering her apparent lack of a torch I thought it quite remarkable that she had managed to make it up the hazardous stone steps without breaking a limb. I was often shocked by the goat-like agility of a scrawny woman of her advanced years, not realising said agility would facilitate her sneaking around in the dark.

Dispensing with the usual polite formality of greetings she immediately demanded if I had any water, saying "*Echete nero*?"

"*Den echo nero, to nero einai svisto,*" I replied, telling her the water was off.

The sound of conversation and laughter drifting outside from the grand salon obviously piqued Maria's curiosity. Pushing rudely past me she barged right in, demanding to know if we were having a pool party. Ever since she became the first non-Brit to make a splash in Harold's swimming pool when I had wangled her first and only invitation, she had been obsessed with the notion that foreigners were excluding her from their frequent pool parties. She appeared so preoccupied with her foolish obsession that it must have slipped her mind that we didn't actually have a pool; in fact Harold's pride and joy was the only swimming pool in the village.

BUCKET TO GREECE (VOL. 2)

I needed Spiros' assistance in translating in order to make head or tail of Maria's rasping words interspersed with high pitched lamentable wails, following the old woman's discovery that she had been excluded from our dinner party. I could hardly ask Spiros to tell her the whole point of the gathering was to dangle eligible bachelors in front of Geraldine and that Kyria Maria didn't quite make the cut, being neither a bachelor nor eligible. If Marigold's intentions became public knowledge it would only embarrass Geraldine and the motley collection of bachelors.

"Tell her not to upset herself," Marigold pleaded, taking me by surprise. Maria's presence usually irritated my wife to distraction yet on this occasion the sight of our neighbour's distress appeared to move her; I suspected she was attempting to portray herself as sympathetic in front of our guests. "Victor, see if the ice cubes have melted enough to give her a glass of water."

"Kyria Maria say she is the shocked to find us all the eating and drinking when she has not the water enough to prepare a simple pan of pasta to eat," Spiros said.

"Oh how terrible," Geraldine exclaimed,

dashing into the kitchen for another plate and some cutlery, saying, "Barry why don't you bring the chair from Victor's office so the poor old dear can join us for a bite to eat."

Even though Maria couldn't possibly understand Geraldine's words, the gleam in her eye made it clear she had successfully manipulated our house guest into setting an extra place at the dinner table. Her bottom had barely made contact with the seat before she was stuffing her mouth with naan bread and spooning the last of the curry onto her plate, declaring the tikka masala to be *"einai poly notsimo."* I needed no translation, I was used to hearing such praise in the taverna and Maria's face clearly expressed her appreciative delight of my delicious cooking as she tucked in with gusto.

Maria's evident enjoyment of the foreign dish surprised me; I had anticipated she would react with the same disgust she had displayed when she'd stuck her fingers into our jar of Marmite. She appeared quite distraught to realise there was no more curry on offer. Dimitris caught Maria staring covetously at his plate of untouched food and reluctantly passed it over to her. I suspected he had planned to somehow sneak it out to the new pig he had purchased with his Millionaire winnings, despite my sound advice on avoiding the unhygienic practice of feeding the creature swill. Even though Maria had not been invited I was pleased that at least one of the Greeks around the table was so thoroughly relishing my culinary offering.

Vangelis excused himself from the table, stepping onto the balcony for a crafty cigarette. Sending a wink in my direction Barry wasted no time in joining the builder. Presuming he was about to broach the subject of going into business together, I crossed my fingers, hoping Vangelis would be receptive to Barry's business proposition. I had a vested interest in the outcome of their chat since Marigold would be ecstatic if her brother was to make the move to Greece; a happy wife meant a quiet life for me. I noticed the two men shaking hands before they returned to the table but decided this was not the appropriate occasion to ask how their chat had gone. Instead I announced to everyone that Barry would be staying on for another week in Greece as he had generously volunteered to give up his time to build me an outdoor bread oven to rival the one Dina used to bake bread for the village.

Marigold's face radiated joy at this unexpected news. Geraldine managed to break eye contact with Spiros for long enough to declare it would be nice to spend a bit of time with Barry now that he would be staying on, suggesting they could perhaps explore the area together. Her comment made me wonder if her apparent interest in Spiros was feigned and if she perhaps still carried a torch for Barry, despite his rejection of her unwanted advances back in Manchester.

Geraldine's suggestion that she and Barry might spend some time together was not well received by Cynthia who placed a hand possessively on my brother-in-law's arm. I couldn't tell from Cynthia's blush if Barry had already shared with her the news that he was staying on for an extra week or if she was just now hearing his plans for the first time. Her simpering smile led me to speculate it was a surprise, and her possessive gesture demonstrated she was publicly staking her claim to Barry to warn Geraldine off. It was the first time I had detected Cynthia's jealous streak.

"Why you to want the archaic contraption outside when you have the modern bread baking machine in the kitchen?" Spiros queried, reminding us all of Barry's supposed reason for extending his visit.

"Aside from its functionality, the traditional aspect of an outside oven with its old world charm appeals to me," I replied.

Spiros stared at me as though I had lost my marbles, scoffingly saying, "You foreigns have the strange notions, we Greeks could not to wait to have the modern conveniences yet you want to replicate the old peasant life."

"I never intended to imply there was anything peasant-like about the traditional Greek way of life," I objected, covering my embarrassment by saying, "Anyone for sherry trifle?"

The Greek guests all perked up at the mention of trifle, realising they need not go home hungry after all if they could down a bowlful of Marigold's delicious dessert, obviously recalling it fondly after sampling it at the house naming ceremony. A sharp rap at the front door made me cringe; there simply wasn't enough trifle to satisfy another uninvited guest. Noticing that my hands were full of dessert bowls Geraldine sprang eagerly to her feet, offering to get the door, making me wonder if Spiros' ardent attentions were not quite as welcome as I had supposed.

Geraldine returned to the room, cornering

me in the kitchen to whisper, "I think it's that chap from the garden this morning, the one under the hosepipe, I can't be sure since he looks different with his clothes on. I left him standing on the doorstep since I can't understand a word he's saying. I know that Marigold isn't too keen and doesn't want to encourage him."

"I'll see to it," I said, hoping I could get rid of Guzim quickly and return to our guests.

The Albanian from the shed wanted to know if we had any water to spare since his hosepipe was dry. I explained that the water was off and we didn't have any either, hopeful he would take the hint to leave from my brusque tone. Unfortunately Guzim seemed inclined to lurk on the doorstep for a chat. I wasn't entirely certain but I think he told me that because I'd been so impressed with his gift of hand knitted mittens from loose rabbit fur that his wife was now knitting an identical pair to send to Fatos Nano, the Albanian prime minister. Somewhere during his spiel my Greek comprehension failed me. Although I could pick out odd words, mobsters and compensation being two, I couldn't work out why he would dream of doing such a thing unless it was the custom in his country to send homemade gifts to government representatives, perhaps in the hope of receiving favours in return. It was likely my translating skills were so inept that I had got the wrong end of the stick; my confused interpretation of whatever Guzim was chuntering on about sounded terribly far-fetched.

Although I was tempted to pop indoors to grab my English to Greek pocket dictionary to explain that the mittens he'd gifted me were riddled with fungal organisms that spread a virulent strain of dermatophytosis, I remembered I had guests. Keeping my own counsel on the wisdom of his possibly spreading dermatophytosis

amongst the higher echelons of the Albanian government I took the easy way out by bribing Guzim to leave with the customary bottle of Amstel.

"What did the Guzim want?" Vangelis enquired on my return. He was obviously suspicious as to the Albanian's motives in calling round, positive in his opinion that Guzim was always trying to pull a fast one.

"Just some water," I replied, not wishing to bore my guests with some convoluted tale about contagious mittens. "He's gone and worked the plank in the fence loose again so he can traipse through the garden."

"Not to worry, the Barry can fix it *avrio*, he is very handy." Vangelis said confidently. Catching my eye Barry gave an imperceptible nod, which I interpreted as Vangelis having expressed interest in his business proposition.

My spoon was inching close to the trifle when there was yet another sharp rap on the front door, indicating we had yet another unwanted caller, or more likely, Guzim was back for another beer.

"It's like Piccadilly Circus this evening," Marigold complained, making no effort to get up.

"I'll go, shall I?" I said to Marigold, my attempt at flippant sarcasm completely lost as it flew over her head. I flung the front door open in annoyance, fully prepared to give Guzim as much of a piece of my mind as my limited grasp of Greek would allow. I was surprised to discover that instead of confronting Guzim. I was about to lay into Papas Andreas, the esteemed clergyman who headed up three local parishes and had officiated at our house blessing ceremony. Hoping he had forgotten my little faux pas about his blessing the house with diarrhoea, I wondered to what we owed this honour.

Apologising for disturbing me he declined my invitation he come in, explaining this wasn't a social call, he was looking for his mother. He was alarmed to discover Kyria Maria was not at home, an unusual state of affairs that had him worried enough to seek to enquire if any of the neighbours had seen her. I was able to assuage his anxiety by assuring him his mother was eating with us.

In measured English Papas Andreas said, "She did not tell me you had invited her to eat with you."

"It was a spur of the moment thing," I replied, reluctant to reveal his mother had gate-crashed our dinner party.

"I not to understand your English," the Papas said.

"Your mother called by to ask if we had water and stayed on for something to eat," I clarified, realising my idiom had confused him.

"I understand now," he said, rolling his eyes, a gesture that demonstrated he was well used to Maria's ways. "You are the kind neighbour Victor. Would you like I should take her home now? It is getting late."

Glancing at my watch I noted it was nearly nine o'clock. I agreed it would be helpful if the

Papas took his mother away as I needed to leave for my shift at the taverna shortly. I worried that despite her goat-like agility she may come a cropper making her way down the hazardous stone steps in the dark.

Papas Andreas followed me through to the grand salon, surprised to see his mother in the midst of such a large gathering. All eyes turned momentarily towards this latest arrival. In turn his eyes scanned the seated guests as he apologised for intruding, saying he was not there to interrupt the festivities, but to collect his mother. I noticed his words faltered abruptly. Following his line of vision I saw that Geraldine had reddened far more than her sunburn, she was clearly blushing. The other guests returned to their conversations and I realised I was perhaps the only one present who was aware of the instant spark of passion between the Papas and Geraldine, a palpable electric current drawing their eyes inexorably together. Geraldine was oblivious to Spiros' attempts to engage her in conversation, her focus riveted on the handsome bearded priest. In turn Papas Andreas appeared to have forgotten all about collecting his mother; rooted to the spot like a religious statue he seemed unable to drag his attention away from the magnetic pull of Geraldine's eyes. Pouring a whiskey, I pressed it onto the Papas, the glass shaking noticeably in his trembling hand before slipping through his fingers, clattering to the floor, shards of glass flying everywhere. Papas Andreas visibly shuddered, the sound of breaking glass drawing him out of his transfixed state.

As I rushed to fetch a dustpan and brush before someone could do themselves an injury on the broken shards, there was yet another loud rap on the front door.

"I'll get it," Marigold offered. "I expect Guzim is back hoping to cadge another Amstel."

"Thank you, I must dispose of this glass safely before I leave for the taverna. I would never live it down if I was to be caught out flouting health and safety guidelines."

Chapter 23

A Harridan in the House

After wrapping the broken shards of glass in newspaper I stacked the used dishes in the kitchen, wondering how long we would remain without water. The prospect of being confronted with a mountain of curry smeared plates the next morning was not one I relished, nor was the thought of confronting an un-flushed toilet or going without my morning shower. I hoped the water would be switched back on so that Marigold and Geraldine could tackle the dishes before I returned. The thought of Geraldine made me ponder the obvious electric spark between her and Papas Andreas; I would discuss it with Marigold later and ask what she thought.

Papas Andreas was no longer in the room although curiously his mother was still at the table, gorging herself on sherry trifle. Geraldine and Marigold were also absent from the room. Spotting the outline of two silhouettes on the balcony I surmised that Geraldine must be stealing a private moment with the cleric. Recalling Marigold had gone out to get rid of Guzim I wondered what could be keeping her. She usually gave the Albanian short shrift, having no patience for his contrived heart-string pulling antics.

The sound of raised voices filtering through from the hallway made me wonder about the cause of this sudden commotion. My hands still full of dishes, I was relieved to see Barry stand up, prepared to go to the aid of his sister. Before he had chance to step into the hallway Marigold returned to the salon looking very uneasy, followed by a complete stranger, an imposing red-haired woman I guessed to be in her late seventies with a determined look plastered on her heavily-made up face.

I looked on in abject horror as the heavyset stranger peering above the rectangular glasses perched on the end of her nose approached Barry, the visions of the featureless bulbous figure that had plagued me in recent months suddenly transformed into a living person. Transfixed, I watched as she threw her arms around Barry in a suffocating embrace, pressing his head into her ample bosom and dramatically crying, "My son, I have found you at last."

Everyone in the room turned to stare, the Greeks who understood English translating the woman's words for those that didn't. Cynthia looked on, her transparent expression showing she was completely mortified that this vulgar looking creature might be Barry's mother. Geraldine stepped in from the balcony, rushing to wrestle Barry from the woman's firm grip, demanding, "What on earth are you doing here? Let him go."

"My son, my son," the woman repeated dramatically, refusing to relinquish her grasp on Barry who was struggling to tear his head free from her chest.

"Marigold, this is the ghastly woman I told you about who caused such a commotion on the plane over from Manchester, the one who said she was staying with family in Greece," Geraldine shouted, attempting to prise Barry free from the woman's arms.

Finally, managing to come up for air, Barry growled, "Let go of me, you harridan."

"She must have got the wrong house, I expect she belongs to that boorish chap with the pool," Geraldine said, still trying to yank Barry loose.

"I'm afraid she belongs to us," Marigold said, her voice barely above a whisper.

"Get off me you deranged lunatic, you are most definitely not my mother," Barry shouted, falling backwards into Geraldine's arms.

"Shame on you, trying to disown me without giving me a chance. I suppose you think I'm an embarrassment, thinking yourself too good for the likes of me with your fancy house," the woman practically spat in Barry's face.

"What on earth is going on Barry, who is this dreadful overbearing woman?" Cynthia asked.

I felt a deep stab of humiliation when I realised everyone was watching the drama unfold with mouths agape, no doubt glad they'd come over since the entertainment was far more riveting than anything Greek television could offer.

Barry looked across at me sheepishly. I could visualise the cogs in his brain whirling as he finally made the connection; I could read the pity etched on his face.

Marigold stepped forward, saying "Victor this is…"

I interrupted her. "I know who it is, it's Violet Burke."

Since the moment this overdone bulbous creature had entered the room I had known instinctively that she was the callous absconded parent who had abandoned me as a baby in a bucket at the railway station. Locking eyes across the room, my steely expression warned her to keep her distance.

Taking a tentative step towards me Violet Burke said, "Victor?" confusing everyone except Marigold and Barry by using the name no one had called me since I was adopted, a name none of my guests recognised.

"I can't abide tardiness and you're more than half a century late," I snapped. Striding through the salon without looking back, I added, "I'm going to be late for work."

Chapter 24

Putting off the Inevitable

A rriving at the taverna I caught Nikos in the act of getting the pig swill together to feed his swine. His disappointment was evident when I didn't remonstrate against this filthy practice. I realised he enjoyed the good-humoured arguments prompted by my hygiene foibles, but I was in no mood to indulge in our usual banter.

I went about my general taverna duties of throwing salads together and frying potatoes, with Dina fussing over me non-stop, obviously sensing something was amiss. Her constant refrain of "*eisai kala*?" as she repeatedly asked if I was all right eventually caused me to snap at her, telling her to stop asking, or at least that's what I thought I had said. Giving me a weary pat on the shoulder Dina went off in search of her husband, returning with Nikos who laughingly asked, "Tell me Victor, why you tell the Dina to stop her nostril, it make not sense? She clip the nose hair last week."

"I must have mixed up my Greek vocabulary," I said, churlishly adding, "It's not as though you never mix up your English."

"But this distemper is not like you Victor," Nikos said.

"See, there you go again mixing up your English. Do I look like a mad dog? Distemper is a contagious canine disease often spread by the unhygienic practice of dogs sharing feeding bowls," I snapped.

"I not know that dog disease word, how you say, distemper, in Greek," Nikos said, distracting me enough from my disjointed mood to make a mental note to look up the Greek word for distemper. The taverna owner continued to press me, saying, "Still, you have the deficient mood. Did the curry dinner not go well?"

"I'd rather not talk about it," I said, turning my back to lower the chip basket into the deep fat fryer. "But do please apologise to Dina for my ill-mannered mood, I didn't mean to upset her."

"She think of you like the son Victor, she will to forgive you," Nikos assured me. Nikos' kind words touched me and I reflected Kostis was a lucky man indeed to have Dina for a mother whilst I'd suffered the frightful bad luck of being spawned by the uncouth harridan now making an exhibition of herself in my living room.

"Ah, here is the Barry. Take ten minutes for the cigarette Victor, I keep the eye on the potatoes," Nikos offered, knowing full well that I don't smoke.

Walking over to Barry I said "*ela exo*," come outside. As we wandered over to perch on the wall Barry tried to lighten the mood by saying, "Your Greek is really coming on well, you just spoke to me in Greek without even realising. You'll be dreaming in Greek before you know it."

"That's what hours of skivvying in a Greek kitchen does," I muttered, appreciative that Barry had sensed I needed his company.

"Don't you mean cheffing?" Barry feebly joked.

"Has everyone left?" I asked, remembering I had abruptly walked out on the guests I had invited to the dinner party. As the host it was quite inexcusable that I had acted in such a rude manner.

"Yes, they all went home when you came here," Barry said. "Spiros and Vangelis were concerned, they were going to follow you over, but Athena told them to leave you be for a while."

"Marigold must hate me. The humiliation at the dinner party, and then leaving her to deal with that Violet Burke person."

"Don't be daft Victor, she's worried about you. I came over rather than Marigold, she didn't want to leave your mother alone in the house and someone had to deal with her," Barry said.

"She looked the type who'd leg it with our best silver," I said.

"You don't have any, do you?" Barry asked rhetorically. "You've had a feeling this would happen."

"Ever since the night I had the phone call to say she'd turned up in Manchester my thoughts have been haunted by an amorphous blob with a shock of red hair," I said, thinking the bulbous creature of my imagination now had features. "She certainly picked her moment, turning up in the middle of a dinner party. What's Marigold going to do with her?"

"Well she couldn't just turn her out onto the village street at this hour, not in a strange country, she had to consider her age," Barry sighed.

"Don't tell me the Burke woman tried to win Marigold's sympathy by playing the feeble old lady card," I snorted derisively, thinking my wife wouldn't stand for that sort of nonsense.

"I think she'd be hard pressed to play the feeble card, she's most definitely a woman of substance," Barry said.

Violet Burke certainly presented as substantial, a solid figure of a woman rather than fat. I'd hazard a guess that the blowsy overdone creature had been a handsome woman in her day.

"So she's still at the house?" I asked.

"What choice did Marigold have, she had to offer her a bed for the night at least," Barry said with a shrug.

"Please don't tell me that Marigold has put her on the sofa-bed in my office," I exclaimed, imagining her rifling through my belongings and devouring the first few chapters of my book.

"Well she tried, but I have to tell you Victor that this Violet woman is no shrinking violet, the offer of the sofa-bed simply wasn't good enough for her. She very bossily insisted that Marigold turf Geraldine out of the best spare bedroom for her. Geraldine has been relegated to the sofa-bed in your office."

"Well where are you going to pretend to sleep then?" I asked, thinking the Burke woman had a cheek.

"I will just have to pretend to sleep on the sofa in the lounge, sorry, the grand salon," Barry said. "I can stay over and sleep on it for real if it would make you feel better having me around."

"No, that's all right, make the most of your time with Cynthia," I told him, thinking there was no reason we all had to suffer.

"To be honest I thought of asking Cynthia if she could squeeze Geraldine in because she was horrified when Violet Burke turned up, having taken an intense dislike to her on the plane ride over because apparently she was obnoxiously loud and vulgar."

"I wouldn't do that if I were you, Cynthia was displaying classic green-eyed signs of jealousy earlier where Geraldine was concerned," I cautioned. "Barry, we picked Geraldine up at noon yesterday in town. If this Burke person was on the same plane and bus as Geraldine, why did it take her another day and a half to show up in Meli?"

"She said she needed a decent night's kip in a proper bed before she suffered another second of travel. She stayed in a hotel up in town last night and then took the bus down to the coast this afternoon. She was hopping mad when there wasn't a bus or taxi to bring her up to the village," Barry explained. Transport links to Meli were sketchy at the best of times, but non-existent in winter.

"Then how did she get up to Meli?" I asked.

"You'd rather not know," Barry said flatly.

"I'm sure I'd rather not, but if there's something you're not telling me you'd better spit it out," I said impatiently.

"Well she went into a bar to see if they could rustle up a taxi for her and she got talking to Harold and Joan. Apparently they all got on like a house on fire and they gave her a lift up to Meli."

My heart sank. I had no idea how indiscreet this Burke person was, but would hazard a guess that Harold and Joan had prised as much information as they could out of her.

"It might not be as bad as you think Victor. Have you ever known Harold let another person get a word in edgeways? Hold on a sec, that's Marigold calling my mobile," Barry said, walking away to try to receive a better reception.

Whilst Barry was speaking to Marigold, Nikos came outside carrying a jacket, a plastic bottle of spitiko wine and a couple of glasses. He placed the old jacket that stank of fried chips around my shoulders, reminding me I had dashed out into the cold December night without grabbing a coat. Putting a hand firmly on my arm he said, "Victor you to have the weight of the world on your head. Take the drink, you look to need it; I finish to fry the potatoes."

"Thank you Niko, that's most kind. I'm sorry that my head is somewhere else tonight," I said, just as Barry returned.

"Marigold needs me to get back, she says she has to have a break from your mother, she's done nothing but carp since she got to the house and apparently she's just had a hissy fit when she discovered you don't have a flushable toilet. Marigold wants to come over here to be with you, but she doesn't feel right about leaving your mother alone. I guess it's my turn to be stuck with her, but you know you will have to face her sometime Victor. You can't put off the inevitable forever," Barry said.

"Do me a favour Barry," I said.

"Anything, you know that."

"Get Nikos to give you a bucket of water to take back with you."

I knew Barry was right and I couldn't put off the inevitable forever, but for now I preferred to sit outdoors in the cold moonless night sipping Nikos' *spitiko*, knowing Marigold would soon be on her way to join me. I may not wish to confront my mother just yet, but at least I could send her a bucket of water to flush the toilet.

Chapter 25

From Bucket to Burke to Blossom

The disconcerting arrival of Violet Burke put a spanner in any hopes I had of a peaceful night's sleep. Sleep proved elusive as I tossed and turned beside Marigold's snoring body, and I couldn't help but dwell on the events of the evening following the unexpected appearance of my absconded parent. Marigold was my rock, in tune with my feelings as she took my hand in hers, joining me on the wall outside the taverna earlier, in spite of the cold. Unable to sleep I replayed the conversation with my wife in my head.

"I'm sorry," I told my wife. "I had to get out of there, I just couldn't face her, but I shouldn't have left you to deal with her. After all, she's my mess to clean up."

"Oh Victor, you have absolutely nothing to apologise for, it must have been a terrible shock for you the way she just turned up out of the blue like that," Marigold said, squeezing my hand tightly.

"Like a burke from the blue," I said.

"I was happy to deal with her, well not exactly happy but you know what I mean, anything rather than see you tormented like that. You looked like you had seen a ghost when she walked in," Marigold stated.

"Ever since she turned up in Manchester I knew beyond a shadow of a doubt that she'd turn up here, I sensed it. I kept having visions of an amorphous blob with no features, I couldn't shake the image. Do you know I even took her featureless head off with the strimmer, imagine, me who has never committed an act of violence in my life. It was easier to deal with her in my imagination than confront her in reality," I admitted.

"I'd better ask Vangelis to store the strimmer away with his other tools; I don't fancy visiting you in a Greek prison cell. The authorities might not look too kindly on matricide, though in your defence I'm sure they might make allowances if they'd actually met your mother," Marigold said in an attempt to lighten my mood. "She's a difficult woman, to put it mildly."

"That chap Gary who bought our house in Manchester warned me she was a bit of a battle-axe," I reminded Marigold.

"That description doesn't even begin to do her justice," Marigold sighed. "She's overbearingly rude and bossy, and I hate to say it, but a tad common. I had no choice but to offer her a bed for the night though, you understand that I couldn't just turf her out Victor. It was dark and she's a pensioner all alone in a strange country. Once she'd agreed to stay she not only demanded Geraldine give up her bed, claiming the sofa-bed looked far too lumpy and uncomfortable, but she demanded I change the sheets because the cats had been in there. She can't abide cats, she made that clear, though I have to say the feeling was mutual, they certainly didn't take to her."

"They do say that cats are excellent judges of character," I said.

"And you wouldn't believe the fuss she made when she discovered we didn't have a bath tub or any water."

"A tub would have been pretty useless with the water off," I pointed out.

"She stayed at a hotel in town last night; you should have heard her carrying on about the rip-off prices. She certainly seems to love to complain, she went on endlessly about her hotel room only having a shower instead of a bath. There were ants crawling all over the washbasin and apparently she can't abide foreign insects,

"Perhaps Catastrophe could be persuaded to drag a lizard into the guest bed," I quipped.

"Don't even joke Victor, I hate to imagine how she'd carry on if she came face to face with a gecko or a lizard, apparently she can't abide foreign creatures, actually she can't abide anything foreign, and she doesn't appear to appreciate overseas travel. She complained it was full of foreigners abroad and…"

"Let me guess," I interrupted, "She can't abide foreigners."

"Well she's quite partial to Americans, but apparently they don't count as foreign because they speak English."

"Well at least something meets with her approval," I said. "I imagine her abhorrence of so many things includes babies, considering how quickly she abandoned me in a bucket at the railway station."

"This will be your chance to find out once and for all Victor, she must have had her reasons. Just think, if she hadn't abandoned you then you would likely have been dragged up by an embittered battle-axe rather than the lovely family who adopted you," Marigold reasoned.

"It's too soon, I'm not ready to hear her excuses," I admitted.

"Victor, you have been waiting fifty-eight years to hear the truth," Marigold pointed out. "Let's walk back now; you've had a bit of time to get used to the idea of facing her."

"You go, Marigold. I'm still not ready to face her yet. Can I ask you to do something for me?"

"Anything Victor, you know that," Marigold said tenderly.

"Pack her off to bed for the night and tell her I don't want to see her until the morning, I have to get used to the idea of her first."

"I'll do that Victor. I'll make sure the coast

is clear before you come home."

As I replayed my conversation with Marigold in my mind I realised I was a lucky man indeed to have such a caring wife, and such a supportive brother-in-law. I was finally drifting into sleep when I was rudely disturbed by the sound of something clattering through the kitchen cupboards and banging the fridge door loudly. Either Clawsome was on the prowl or Violet Burke was not too covertly enjoying a post-midnight snack.

Donning my dressing gown and slippers I shuffled through to the kitchen where I discovered Violet Burke clad in an ugly fuchsia dressing gown that looked as though it had been hacked from an old candlewick bedspread. She looked every inch the harridan, the fuchsia clashing hideously with her garishly dyed red hair. She was in the act of slipping one of my prized Fray Bentos steak and kidney pies into the oven whilst helping herself to my best Metaxa. Eyeing me above the narrow rectangular spectacles perched on the end of her nose, as though I was the interloper in my own kitchen, the Burke woman wordlessly slopped some brandy into an extra glass and slid it across to me. Fortunately something in my stance must have warned her I would not tolerate one of the suffocating embraces she had subjected Barry to.

"I found the Fray Bentos lurking at the back of the cupboard. How you can expect your guests to eat all this foreign muck without coming down with something nasty is beyond me," Violet Burke said. I considered her words an odd conversation starter from a mother who had not as yet formally introduced herself to her long lost son, yet they served as an ice breaker between us. "I can't even pronounce most of the stuff in your fridge, let alone work out what to do with it. What's this, it looks like something you've wiped up from a grubby canteen floor?" she sneered.

"That's *tirokafteri*, a spicy feta cheese dip. I made it myself," I replied haughtily.

"That Marigold's got you right under the thumb, having you doing the cooking," she said dismissively.

"I happen to enjoy experimenting in the kitchen," I retorted.

Eyeing a jar of Kalamata olives suspiciously she opined, "I suppose now I'm part of a posh family I should be putting these in my drink. Personally I prefer a nice silver skin pickle in my beverage."

Without deigning to reply I passed her a jar of miniature silver skin onions we'd brought over from England, wincing in horror as she threw a handful of them into her glass of five start brandy, ignoring the toothpicks I proffered to use as cocktail sticks.

"Ooh Tesco, very posh, it's a bit more up-market than Spar. It's nice to see you appreciate the good brands," she said.

She had a point; you couldn't beat a Tesco pickle I thought, reaching across for the jar, spooning some onto a plate and adding a thick slice of Greek graviera cheese, defiant of the heartburn the combination would inevitably trigger at this late hour.

"Did you do the washing-up?" I asked, noticing that all the curry smeared plates and trifle bowls from the dinner party that had been piled up in the kitchen when I returned from the taverna were now drying in the dish rack. I couldn't imagine that Geraldine had slipped out of bed to tackle the dishes.

"If there's one thing I can't abide it's a filthy kitchen or the slovenly habit of letting dirty dishes pile up in the sink. I gave them a thorough washing as soon as the water came back on. They took a right old scrubbing, full of congealed curry they were. Personally I can't be doing with foreign curry. We sell curry sauce in the chippy to go on the side, but I never touch it. I can't understand why folks bother with it when there are mushy peas on the go. You can't beat a chip barm with a filling of mushy peas," Violet Burke pronounced.

I was gratified that I wouldn't need to face a mound of dirty dishes the next morning, surprised that the Burke woman appeared to share my exacting hygiene standards.

"I think it's time you told me about my father," I said, sitting down across from her at the table and taking a large slug of brandy to prepare myself for what horrors she may reveal. It was too soon to hear her excuse for abandoning me in a bucket and naturally I was curious about my father.

"Well I did name you after your fathers," she said.

"Fathers, as in more than one?" I spluttered. "How is that even possible?"

"I blame it on the blackout and the shortage of nylons," she said. "You couldn't get nylons or chocolate until the Yanks turned up in Warrington."

"Warrington?" I asked, trying to recall if there was a railway connection between Warrington and Manchester back in 1944.

"Well Burtonwood to be precise, the place was crawling with Yanks on account of the air force base. I scrubbed up well back in the day, I had a fine figure and the fellows were a sucker for a busty redhead with a neat set of pins. I was pretty sure your father was Ulysses; I met him when I snuck into the Casino Ballroom through the fire escape and we hit it off right away. He was an arse end Charlie," Violet Bucket revealed.

"I really think details like that are inappropriate," I sniffed at her vulgar turn of phrase.

"Oh get off your high horse, an arse end Charlie was what we called the rear gunners, you certainly have a filthy mind for someone who looks as though they've got a pickle stuck up his arse. Ulysses was a dab hand with the trumpet. I had hopes he'd take me back to Mississippi with him after the war, but then I got the biggest shock when you didn't come out black. I did wonder if you might darken up, but I can see that you haven't. I'd been convinced Ulysses was the one that got me up the spout, but then you came out so pallid I had to scrub his name off the list and work out who else I'd been a bit free with. I managed to narrow it down to either Donnie or Vic, but that's as far as I got, you didn't come out with a striking resemblance to either of them. That's why I put their names on your hat, as a clue like."

"You mean the names attached to that totally inappropriate pink frilly bonnet," I countered.

"I was expecting to birth a black girl; you can't imagine the shock when I had a white boy."

"So the names on the bonnet weren't the names you gave me, they were the names of my possible fathers?" I clarified. "You do realise you landed me with the initials of VD with all its unfortunate disease riddled connotations? My humiliation was compounded when I was saddled with the surname Bucket after the metal receptacle you abandoned me in. Even though Burke isn't exactly glorious it would have been less debasing than Bucket."

"But I wasn't a Burke back then, I was a Blossom," Violet Burke protested.

I ran this new gem through my mind, thinking

my unknown grandparents must have been blessed with a sense of humour to name their Blossom offspring Violet. I reflected that the name V.D. Blossom would no doubt have led to even more ribald jokes about blossoming warts or genital itches. The surname was a tad too girly for a man; suddenly Bucket didn't seem quite so bad in comparison.

"I thought it would be nice if you were named after your fathers, though Ulysses might have been a bit more your style seeing as though you have a fondness for Greek things," she said.

"So Ulysses was Greek? A black Greek trumpet player from Mississippi?" I was totally confused now.

"I never said he was Greek, he had a Greek name, but for all I know he might have had a bit of Greek blood in him. He did have lovely manners, is that a Greek thing? Anyway I couldn't expect him to take me home with him. I could hardly pass a white Jewish baby off as his, not when he was so dark. They were still very big on segregation in the south at the time."

"So you're telling me I'm Jewish?" I said, reeling in shock.

"Well you could be, do you find yourself breaking into a bit of Yiddish, or riddled with angst?"

"I wasn't angst ridden until you turned up and no, I don't speak Yiddish, it's hard enough getting to grips with Greek," I said.

"Oh that's a pity; Donnie was a nice Jewish boy from Brooklyn, being a boffin he was a cut above the usual bods, but he couldn't half make me laugh. He was a bit on the short side now I think of it; his eyes were level with my cleavage, whereas Vic was very tall, like you."

"Vic?" I said, wondering how many more names she was going to dangle in front of me. "And which part of the good old US of A did Vic hail from?"

"Oh he wasn't a Yank, I think he came from Crewe, but he was a bit cagey about his background. He moved around a lot being a travelling salesman. He said he'd been discharged from the army on medical grounds but I didn't really buy it, he limped on a different leg every time I saw him. I'd a feeling he'd gone AWOL, but what with the rationing I couldn't afford to be too fussy, a girl had to have soap."

This was sounding worse by the moment. It appeared that Violet Burke, or rather Blossom, had been a bit of a slapper who'd been rather free with her favours in exchange for a bar of soap and a pair of nylons. It seemed that of the three, so far mentioned, possible suspects linked to my paternity, one was ruled out as I wasn't black and the second sounding unlikely due to him being very short. Either of them sounded preferable to a possibly dishonourable army deserter.

"Vic was a bit of a strange one really, he had the gift of the gab when he wanted, but he could be a bit stuffy. To be honest it was a bit insulting the way he had to scour his hands after we'd had a bit of a tumble. He was obsessed with hygiene and germs, probably why it suited him selling soap."

I didn't like the sound of this. A tall man with a way with words and a hygiene obsession sounded a bit too familiar for comfort. I don't know what triggered my next question. I can only presume some latent snobbery inherited through my paternal genes made me blurt out, "Did he at least sell a decent brand of soap like Pears?"

"Good grief no, nothing as posh as Pears. He sold blocks of laundry soap door-to-door, the rough type that you had to grate into the dolly tub. He gave me huge slabs of the stuff and I washed my hair with it, I was that glad when rationing ended because it gave me terrible dandruff. Dandruff is never a good look on a red head. Vic always stank of laundry soap, like I said he was obsessed with hygiene, I've never known anyone wash more than he did. Are you into washing a lot?"

"Well certainly I like to shower on a regular basis and of course in my line of work a high standard of personal hygiene is always expected," I said.

"What line of work is that then?"

"A public health inspector."

"One of them blithering nuisances always complaining when we don't wash the old ketchup out of the bottom of the Heinz bottles before we fill them up with a cheaper brand in the chip shop, and always barging in demanding to know how often we change the chip fat," she accused indignantly.

"Marrying bottles is a dubious practice, not recommended from a sanitary aspect," I advised." It would be made illegal if I had any say in the matter."

Suddenly realising we'd drifted away from the point of the conversation I asked, "So are you saying you think this limping soap salesman who had possibly absconded from the army was my father, or were there any more contenders for the title that you haven't yet mentioned?"

"You can drop that sarcastic tone. You needn't try and make out I was a bit of a scrubber, Vic was the one always scrubbing his hands," Violet Burke snapped before narrowing her eyes above her spectacles and pensively saying, "You youngsters have no idea what it was like living with rationing and bombs being dropped every minute. Morals got a bit loose with the prospect of death looming round every corner and we grabbed a good time when we could. From the dates I narrowed it down to three possible fellows that might have got me pregnant, and then I ruled out Ulysses on account of your colour. I'd say now that I've met you that you definitely have something of Vic about you, and you're very tall like him. It's a pity; I quite fancied having a Jewish son. My third husband Lionel was Jewish, full of chutzpah, I told him all about you and we tried to find you, but drew a blank."

I was surprised to hear that she'd confided her shameful secret and even more surprised to hear that she'd tried to find me.

"When was that? When you tried to find

me?" I asked.

"That would have been back in sixty-six. I was about to turn forty and Lionel was that keen to have a nipper, but nothing happened. When he accused me of being infertile the truth came out. He really wanted to find you and give you a good home. He was that keen to walk you to school and take you out for ice-cream, he could get a bit sentimental could Lionel, full of schmaltz he was."

"I was twenty-two years old in sixty-six. I hardly needed taking out for ice-cream or walking to school," I said incredulously.

"Well I might have knocked the odd ten or twelve years off my age, so in theory you'd only have been ten." Violet Bucket admitted, finally looking shamefaced for the first time since I'd met her. I shuddered to think how she'd planned to pass her twenty-two year old offspring off as a ten-year-old boy without exposing her lies, if they'd managed to find me.

"I dropped the idea of finding you when Lionel went and got that trollop pregnant in the back row of the Odeon, it left me strapped being on my own again like, cash strapped that is, but it was nothing new. Can you believe the trollop only went and had triplets, Lionel got a bit more than he bargained for with three nippers?"

The smell of burning Fray Bentos tin distracted us from the conversation. Violet Bucket rescued the pie from the oven, competently taking the lid off with a single turn of the tin opener. Without asking she divided the flaky pie into two, piling one half on a plate in front of me.

"Eat up Vic, you're too scrawny. Yes, I think if I had to put money on it I'd say that Vic was definitely your father."

Chapter 26

Warrington Eggs

Sleep yet again proved elusive following my post-midnight conversation with Violet Burke. My ignominious start in life had not featured heavily in my thoughts since my failed attempt to locate my absconded mother following Benjamin's birth, only stirred up once again when Violet Burke had turned up in Manchester just after we'd moved to Greece. In the space of three months I had gone from being a Bucket to a Burke, and now it turned out I had been a Blossom all along. At least there was consistency to my original initials.

As I tossed and turned I reflected that the bucket coincidences that had cropped up throughout my life, which I had interpreted as serendipity, may just have been wishful thinking. The most momentous of course had been my chance meeting with Marigold in a branch of B & Q, both desperate to get our hands on the last galvanised bucket on sale. I had forfeited my claim on the bucket in favour of a first date with the Titian haired beauty I married just five months later.

I have always considered my last big professional promotion to be blessed by the bucket coincidence, another example of serendipity at play. The gruelling three-day job interview process took place in a hotel, where part of the challenge was to spot any breaches of health and safety regulations whilst remaining incognito. Whilst lurking in the corridors to spot any dodgy practices pertaining to room service delivery I was surprised to spot a gentleman bearing a remarkable resemblance to the innovative guitar player known professionally as 'Buckethead'. Although he carried a guitar, I wasn't entirely convinced it was him without the trademark Kentucky Fried Chicken bucket on his head, and I struggled to imagine what he would be doing in such a place since it was hardly the Ritz. Later that same day I spent a frustrating half-hour stuck in a broken lift with him, the boredom only alleviated when 'Buckethead' strummed the blues. I considered it would be far too boorish to invade his privacy and ask for his autograph, so the encounter remained a 'was it' 'wasn't it' moment reminiscent of the old Harmony hairspray television advertisement. When I relayed my tale of being trapped in a lift with the musical celebrity everyone doubted my lift companion had been the real thing, saying there was no mention of Buckethead visiting England in the press. Nevertheless I considered it to be a fortuitous encounter as the very next day I received my prestigious promotion.

I wondered if I would have looked for similar blossom coincidences to interpret as serendipity if I'd known all along I was a Blossom. Fortunately my adoptive parents ditched the names of Victor Donald that had been pencilled on the piece of cardboard, safety-pinned to the pink frilly bonnet tied securely to my head on the night I was found abandoned in a bucket, all too aware of the unsavoury connotations of venereal disease associated with my given initials. My adoptive name was carefully selected to ensure it had no embarrassing associations and my new surname began with a letter far removed from B.

Finally I must have drifted into sleep. The next thing I knew the early morning light was streaming into the bedroom and there was no sign of Marigold in the bed beside me, an unusual state of affairs. My late night encounter with Violet Burke had caused me to sleep past sunrise. A dull pain in my chest made me wonder if Violet Burke's saga had touched my heart, but remembering the post-midnight Fray Bentos pie I reached for a bottle of indigestion remedy. I was relieved to see we still had water though the pressure was little more than a trickle. A slow dripping hot shower revived me before I made my way through to the kitchen where I discovered Violet Burke cooking breakfast, an open bottle of Amstel to hand.

"I'm doing Warrington eggs," she announced.

"Warrington eggs?" I questioned, not being familiar with this northern delicacy.

"Pickled Scotch eggs coated in black pudding

dipped in beer batter and then deep fried," she explained. I was relieved to hear the Amstel had gone in the batter rather than being Violet Burke's choice of breakfast tipple. "We do a roaring trade in them in the chippy but I don't think they're famous outside my patch of Warrington. I smuggled some over in my suitcase, thinking it wouldn't do to trust any of that foreign food you have over here," Violet Burke explained.

"I'll give them a try," I agreed.

"I think I'll pass," Marigold said, scrunching her face up in a picture of disgust. "And you should think of your cholesterol Victor, deep fried pickled eggs wrapped in black pudding will likely play havoc with your levels."

"I might have known you were one of them health food nuts," Violet Burke accused Marigold, looking her up and down over the top of her spectacles with a disparaging stare. "I suppose it's down to you that the cupboards are full of muesli, you should give your husband a proper cooked breakfast."

"Victor and I prefer to follow a healthy diet of muesli and fresh bread with olive oil," Marigold replied.

"Phhh, I've never been on a diet in my life

and I'm as fit as a fiddle at seventy-seven. A bit of cholesterol gets you going in the morning."

Just then Geraldine wandered into the kitchen and Violet Burke demanded, "Will you be wanting some deep fried Warrington eggs or are you another one that prefers a bowl of that bird seed muck they pass off as muesli instead of proper food?"

"There's no need to make fun of my job as a pet food taster, Victor can tell you all about it being a noble career. Anyway I don't have time for breakfast, I'm off to church. I'll see you later Marigold," Geraldine said, buttoning her coat and heading outdoors.

"That's a bit odd; I never had Geraldine down as the religious type," my wife remarked, her words reminding me I hadn't had the chance to discuss with her the electric current that had sparked between Geraldine and Papas Andreas when their eyes had locked in passion the previous evening. I suspected Geraldine's sudden religious conversion was inspired by a totally inappropriate lust for the bearded cleric rather than godly devotion, though I reflected the priest had appeared equally smitten.

Violet Burke plonked a plate of deep fried Warrington eggs in front of me. They were surprisingly good, much tastier than my usual bowl of muesli.

"You look tired Victor," Marigold observed. "I'm glad you went back to bed for a bit of a lie-in. You must have been up at the crack of dawn to get through all that washing-up from last night."

"I can't abide dirty dishes piled up in the sink," Violet Burke said without taking credit for cleaning the dishes.

"You have that in common with Victor then," my wife observed.

"Violet Burke did the dishes," I said, suddenly wondering how I was meant to address her. Mrs Burke sounded much too formal and Violet too familiar. As though reading my thoughts Violet Burke said, "You can call me Vi if you like, it might sound a bit odd if you started calling me mother."

"Indeed, it is much too soon for that, you can't just turn up after being on the missing list for six decades and expect me to call you mother."

"I meant it would sound odd to me, I've never had any practice at this mothering lark. Now finish your eggs before they go cold," she said in a surprisingly maternal tone.

Trying out the new salutation for size Marigold turned to Violet Burke, saying, "Vi, you said last night that you were keen to find Victor so I'm curious why it took you three months to turn up here once you had our address."

"It's not as if I could just jump on the ninety-two bus and pop round, you'd flitted abroad. And passports don't just grow on trees even if I hadn't had to do double shifts in the chippy to save up for the ticket over," Violet Bucket said.

I was surprised to learn that instead of being comfortably pensioned off Violet Burke was still holding down a job in a chip shop. I hoped Marigold wouldn't start up again with all that nonsense about demanding a DNA test to prove the Burke woman wasn't an imposter seeking a cosy billet in her old age. I didn't need a DNA test to confirm the relationship; I knew instinctively that I shared her genes.

"That's another thing you have in common, you both cook chips for a living," Marigold quipped.

"I thought you said you had a fancy job for the council. Did they sack you?" Violet Burke accused. "I expected you'd have done better for yourself than ending up like me, it's a bit of a disappointment to find out you fry chips for a living too."

"I don't do it for a living, I'm helping out in a local taverna because the owner's wife is temporarily incapacitated," I stated.

"It's more of a hobby for Victor," Marigold explained.

"I like to keep busy since I took early retirement from my career as a public health inspector," I clarified, wondering if I might have been doomed to follow in Violet Burke's footsteps if she hadn't abandoned me to be adopted.

"I always said those health inspectors were on a cushy number," Violet Burke scoffed. "Fancy being retired at your age, you're not even sixty yet."

Over the course of the morning Violet Burke revealed the events that had led to her abandoning me. Raised in an impoverished family, she had no expectations beyond a life of domestic servitude. At nineteen years old Violet Blossom found herself having an unexpectedly good war, working by day in a munitions factory near Warrington whilst discovering her striking looks made her exceedingly popular with the Yanks by night. All that changed when she found herself pregnant and unwed. She was keen to start a new life in Mississippi with

Ulysses after the war, but her dreams were shattered when word that she had been a bit free with her favours reached his ears. He refused to put a ring on her finger until he could be sure he was the one responsible for her now visible bump. Single and pregnant, Violet Blossom gave up her work in the factory, knowing her fake wedding ring wasn't fooling anyone.

"It wasn't just the shame and the stigma of being unwed and pregnant, I could have stuck out the gossip; after all half the ones gossiping were no better, they just hadn't got caught out the same so they didn't end up with a reputation for being loose. The thought of all those chemicals in the factory made me pack it in, I didn't want you coming out with three heads," she explained.

I felt grateful that she'd had the good sense not to expose me to dangerous chemicals before I was born. Her three-headed fears may have been ungrounded, but there were well documented cases of munitions factory workers giving birth to bright yellow babies.

"I got a job in a chippy and it wasn't all bad, they handed out free cod liver oil and an extra pint of milk under the Vitamin Welfare Scheme. It's no wonder you turned out so tall."

"I thought it was because I'd inherited the height gene from my soap salesman father," I said, noting that my mother was tall for a woman.

Ignoring my interruption Violet Burke continued her tale, telling me, "I thought you'd be my contribution to the war effort, they were big on encouraging babies, but the District Nurse was a stuck-up harridan who looked down on me like I was a slapper just because I wasn't respectably married. There was no way they were shipping me off to one of those horrible homes for unmarried mothers when my family disowned me. I was at my wits end wondering what to do, hoping with everything I had that once you were born Ulysses would propose. Before I knew it I was giving birth in the back of the chippy with my friend Mabel helping me out. I swore her to secrecy of course, but she never had the chance to blab because she got hit by a bomb when she went home to Oldham that Christmas."

Violet Burke paused in her tale to dab at her eyes with a piece of kitchen roll, obviously still moved by Mabel's terrible fate. Pulling herself together she continued.

"When you didn't come out black I knew that

was the end of things between me and Ulysses, there wasn't going to be any new life in America. Donnie had already been shipped back to the States after getting wounded and I'd no clue how to find him. Vic, the soap salesman, had done a moonlight flit when he got wind the military police were closing in on him for going AWOL. I didn't have two farthings to rub together and I couldn't bring you up with the stigma of having an unmarried mother. Times were different back then, they weren't handing out council flats and a pot of money to unwed mothers, and I couldn't exactly pick up a new fellow who'd be willing to take me on with a baby in tow."

"It must have been hard for her Victor," Marigold said in my mother's defence. "She was only nineteen, abandoned by the scoundrel who got her pregnant and with no support from her family."

I finally had the chance to ask something I'd always wondered about. "What date was I born?"

"The fourteenth of December," my mother replied, her answer finally giving me an actual birthday to celebrate.

"You kept me for five days," I stated, recalling

the actual date I had been discovered in the railway station.

"I didn't want to give you up but I couldn't keep you, not with no money and no idea when the war would end." Tears rolled freely down her face as she spoke and her features softened. I realised the overbearing harridan that had turned up the night before actually had feelings and it had genuinely grieved her to abandon me.

"I knew anyone would give you a better life than I could so I took the pragmatic approach and left you somewhere public."

"But in a bucket," I remonstrated.

"It was either that or the chip fryer basket and we couldn't spare that," she said. I ruminated that of the two options it would have been far more ignominious to have been discovered abandoned in a chip fryer basket, covered in grease and smelling like a chip shop. A smattering of coal dust sounded preferable.

Chapter 27

The Scarlet Woman of Meli

My mother's revelations were interrupted by the sound of someone knocking on the front door. I was relieved when Vi went to deal with the caller, glad of a private moment alone with Marigold to share a tender embrace. Vi returned to the room, announcing she'd seen off the toothless tinker caller with a flea in his ear.

"You want to watch what you put out on your washing line Marigold, with common thieves like him hanging around."

Marigold and I exchanged a confused look. We had both naturally assumed the toothless caller must have been Guzim, but whilst he had a deserved reputation as a scrounger there had never been even a hint of thievery associated with his name.

"I think you are speaking of Guzim, the Albanian who lives in the shed at the bottom of our garden. I can assure you he is honest," I stated."

"Well how else did he get hold of Harold's shirt then if he didn't steal it? I'd recognise it anywhere. Harold was wearing it in the bar yesterday, it has a big Union Jack on the front and a very distinctive tomato ketchup stain," Vi said adamantly. "He's a bit of a funny one that Harold, he told me all about your next door neighbour tinkling in his swimming pool and then he invited me round to swim in it. Disgusting, can you credit it?"

Amused as I was by my mother declining Harold's pool invitation, my immediate concern was catching up with Guzim.

"Guzim may be a nuisance at times but I can assure you that he is no thief, in fact he's my gardener," I said firmly, dashing off in pursuit of him. It wouldn't do if my mother had insulted him so much that he downed tools and refused to dig the vegetable patch. Catching up with Guzim in the garden I apologised for my guest's rudeness. Guzim was shaking from what he described as a terrifying encounter with the old battle-axe, but luckily he had not understood whatever insults my mother had hurled at him. I explained that my guest, I wasn't yet ready to admit to all and sundry that my guest was my mother, was concerned about how he came to be wearing Harold's shirt.

It transpired that the Albanian had no idea the shirt had belonged to Harold. Guzim explained the shirt was a lucky find. He had spotted it lying on top of the bags of rubbish in the public bins, a fortunate discovery indeed since he hadn't even needed to rummage through the foul bags of garbage to come across it; it was there for any passer-by to grab. I reflected that Harold must be profligate as well as ignorant if he cast away a perfectly good shirt at the first sign of a ketchup stain which could have been removed quite easily with the application of a suitable detergent. I also considered things must be bad for Guzim if he was reduced to rescuing discarded ketchup stained clothes from the bins.

Remembering that Guzim now had an extra

mouth to feed, his new-born son Fatos named in honour of the Albanian prime minister, I extended an altruistic gesture by offering him an extra shift in the garden. Sinking to his knees in gratitude, Guzim grasped my knees, offering effusive thanks for the extra work in indecipherable guttural Albanian. By now of course I was used to Guzim's melodramatic antics. I reminded him that Nikos needed help with his olive harvest and I would consider it a personal favour if he took the work since Nikos was getting on in years and was far too proud to ask again. Complaining that Nikos was a slave driver, Guzim prefaced his mutterings with expletives, finally relenting when I bribed him with the offer of a daily Amstel for the duration of his olive picking stint.

On my return Marigold suggested a stroll around the village to walk off the Warrington eggs. Violet Burke declined the offer to join us, saying, "Seeing as you've insisted I stop here I won't be able to settle until I've given the place a good bottoming, it's full of filthy cat hairs, not to mention piles of dead mosquitos under my bed. I can't abide a slovenly house."

Marigold, visibly bridling at the insinuation that she was a slovenly housekeeper, bit her lip.

Although she always attempted to maintain my exacting standards of cleanliness, in truth she loathed housework, finding it a tedious chore. She had tried to persuade me to hire a cleaner but I pointed out their hourly rate was likely more than I earned in the taverna. Pointing Violet Burke in the direction of the mop and my extensive range of cleaning products, Marigold whispered, "I wonder if that's where you get your hygiene obsession from."

"I am not obsessed," I insisted. "I merely have exacting standards."

We were just heading down the stone steps when Violet Burke stuck her head out of the front door, calling out, "Can you pick me up a tin of mushy peas while you're out; I've a terrible craving for a chip barm tonight."

"I'm afraid they don't sell mushy peas in Greece," I called up to her.

"Vi, you can come along to the taverna with me this evening. Victor will be working so you'll have the chance to sample his chips," Marigold shouted.

"As long as they don't come with any foreign muck," my mother called down.

"Well the chicken will be Greek, but I can promise you the best chips you'll ever taste," I assured her. Remembering her exacting hygiene standards I thought it best to warn her that the local taverna was a bit spit and sawdust.

"I'd best bring the mop and Marigolds along with me then," she said pragmatically.

As Marigold and I strolled along the cobbled street I noticed that Meli resembled a picture postcard of a typical Greek village bathed in winter sunshine, the olive trees weighed down with ripe fruit waiting to be picked. The usual crew of elderly village men playing *tavli* outside the village shop were wrapped up in thick winter clothing, warming their hands on their miniature cups of strong Greek coffee. In contrast we basked in the unseasonably warm temperatures, delighted to have escaped yet another damp and dreary Manchester winter.

Dina came out of the shop and rushed to greet us, showering me with kisses as though she hadn't seen me for months, my surly mood of the previous evening already forgiven and forgotten.

"*Eisai kala*?" she trilled, asking me if I was all right.

"*Ola einai kala tora*," I replied, assuring her

everything was good now as I swept her off her feet and spun her around. Her pleasant features were transformed by the warm smile of happiness my spontaneous gesture prompted and she went on her way with a spring in her step.

Marigold tucked her arm into mine and we continued our stroll, stopping to exchange greetings with Dimitris, his nose buried in a book on his doorstep. I experienced a surge of inner excitement when I shared with Dimitris that it turned out that we had the exact same birthdate of December fourteenth 1944 and we would both reach fifty-nine years of age the next weekend.

"It is not the wonder why we are so sympatico Victor, it is the blessed coincidence," Dimitris said.

"It truly is," I agreed.

Dimitris then promptly aged me one year by saying, "If we calculate our age by the Greek way of adding the one extra year then we will be the sixty next weekend."

"I think in this instance you should stick to British time," Marigold advised. I made a mental note to research if the Greek way of adding an extra year was typically European or simply a quirky Greek practice.

Resuming our walk we caught up with Milton and Edna. Feeling bad that because neither of them were eligible bachelors we hadn't included them in the dinner party, I decided to invite them round for elevenses the next morning, making a mental note to bake an extra lemon drizzle for them to take home.

"That's very decent of you old chap, we'll be there," Milton enthused, thanking me for the kindling I'd had Guzim drop off.

"How's the book coming along?" I asked.

"It's coming along like the blazes. I find whenever I hit a spot of writer's block that I only need to look at Edna to feel inspired," Milton said. Marigold ducked down, ostensibly to fasten her shoelace but in reality to hide the laughter I knew she was trying desperately to conceal at the thought of Edna inspiring Milton's erotic musings.

"Oh Milton," Edna said, her face suffused in a bright red blush.

"I was meaning to ask your advice old chap," Milton continued.

"Ask away," I replied.

"Do you have an opinion on the use of non de plumes? Edna thinks it could be a tad embarrassing if people get the wrong idea and think

I'm writing smutty porn."

"I am of the opinion that the use of a non de plume is very sensible," I said. "You don't want to risk being mobbed by fans and a pseudonym is a marvellous way to preserve your anonymity."

"Excellent, excellent. I've been toying with the names Savannah and Scarlett. I can't decide between them, they both sound suitably racy," Milton revealed.

"I think Scarlett is a wonderful choice, it hints that your volume of erotica has been penned by a scarlet woman and it could be a good marketing ploy," I advised, struggling to keep a straight face.

Milton and Edna were barely out of sight when Marigold grabbed my hand, pulling me into a leafy lane where we both collapsed in laughter.

"It's too much. Milton is the scarlet woman of Meli," I quipped.

"Oh Victor, you are a wit."

"I'm glad he's decided not to write under his own name," I said, amused by the thought Meli was turning into an anonymous retreat for incognito writers.

"And you Victor, will you be sticking with

the pen name of V.D. Bucket now you know the truth about your origins?" Marigold asked.

"Strictly speaking I'm actually V.D. Blossom, but considering the serendipity surrounding bucket I shall stick with it. There have been many fortuitous events over the years that I believed I was a Bucket, perhaps the name will prove to be equally fortuitous for my book," I said.

"About your writing Victor," Marigold said hesitantly.

"Don't tell me you want me to give it up? It was your and Barry's idea in the first place."

"Oh not at all, but I've been thinking, perhaps when you've finished penning your moving abroad book you could write a novel based on the life of Violet Burke. Just think what a fascinating life she's lived, working in a munitions factory during wartime. It would give you the opportunity to find out her life story and I know just how much you love a bit of research. I expect you'd find it very cathartic."

"And I'm sure Milton would be happy to divulge his wartime experiences too, I could weave them into the story," I said, already enthused by the idea. "Of course it would involve delving deeper into my mother's story."

"She's here all week," Marigold reminded me.

Chapter 28

Plain Sailing Ahead

When Marigold and I finally recovered our composure we resumed our stroll through the village. As we passed the church we glanced inside, noticing Geraldine deep in what appeared to be an intimate conversation with Papas Andreas. Marigold was about to step into the church to join her friend when I stopped her, pulling her to one side to ask if she'd noticed the immediate spark that had flared between Geraldine and the Papas the previous evening.

"Don't talk daft Victor, he's a priest for goodness sake, and have you seen the state of his bushy beard? I told you we should have got him a beard trimmer for the house blessing ceremony, he's definitely in need of a bit of grooming."

"He may be a priest but he's still a man, and most likely a red-bloodied one at that. He was staring at Geraldine very passionately last night," I said.

"Well she did look very nice, the green powder toned down her sunburn and her hair is always glossy from so much dog food," Marigold replied.

"But you didn't notice that they appeared besotted with each other?" I asked. "Oh I remember now, you'd gone to answer the door when it happened, you must have missed it. It's a rum state of affairs."

"But I had high hopes for her and Spiros, I thought they appeared to be getting on well," Marigold said.

"She lost all interest in him the moment Papas Andreas turned up," I revealed.

"Well fancy that, she does tend to always go for unsuitable men. I suppose you'd better do some research Victor and find out if that kind of thing is allowed in the Orthodox Church. You may have got it all wrong; she may just have caught the religious bug. I'll have a chat with her later, believe me if the priest has taken her fancy I'll hear all about it, Geraldine is nothing if not indiscreet," Marigold said.

Backing away from the church entrance in case Geraldine thought we were spying on her, I decided to share with my wife the news that Barry was considering making the move to Greece.

"But please don't tell him I've told you. He doesn't want to disappoint you if nothing comes of it. It's likely he will go into partnership with Vangelis, but he will need somewhere to live," I said.

After the way Barry had expressed his support for me and the way Marigold had put up with my mother the previous evening, allowing me time to come to terms with her sudden appearance, I realised that if Marigold wanted to invite Barry to live with us permanently I was fine with it, and told her so.

"I expect if Barry does make the move he will choose to live with Cynthia," Marigold said. "They may even get married, it wouldn't surprise me."

"Cynthia's place is only rented, Barry did wonder about converting our downstairs storage," I said.

"*Siga siga*, it's early days", my wife said pragmatically, obviously not wanting to get her hopes up just in case Barry didn't make the move. "Oh look there's Spiros, he does look rather glum. I hope it isn't because Geraldine gave him the brush-off."

Spiros was heading across the village square towards his hearse, looking rather down in the mouth.

"The bad news, another the uncle has died," Spiros said mournfully. After accepting our sympathies he said, "The good news is I inherit the house. He live in the next village over, but difficult I think now to find the people to buy it at this time of year. You know anyone who want the house to buy?"

Marigold and I looked at each other, reading each other's mind, wondering if this could be a serendipitous moment for Barry.

"I can't think of anyone," Marigold told Spiros before he hurried off to the hearse.

"We can mention it to Barry of course, but really the next village is a bit too far away, I'd love to have him just around the corner like we did in Manchester," Marigold said.

"Or just downstairs," I suggested.

We turned towards one of the unpaved lanes that wound up through the village, offering spectacular views down to the sea. As we ambled upwards Marigold raised the topic of my mother, saying, "I hope it was all right asking her along to the taverna this evening, she's sure to embarrass you. If you hate the thought of having her in the house perhaps we could put her up in a hotel for the week, or if it's all too much for you we can always drive her back to the bus station in town. I really wasn't sure what you wanted to do with her."

"She has a flight back to England booked next Saturday from Athens, she has to get back to the chip shop," I said. "One week will give us the chance to get acquainted, yet offer light at the end of the tunnel."

"Geraldine flies back next Saturday too, imagine if they are on the same flight considering how much they loathed each other on sight," Marigold said, attempting to suppress a girlish giggle. "They'll probably kill each other."

An idea struck me.

"How about if I ask Nikos to get someone to cover for me in the taverna at the weekend? I'm sure he can rope Litsa in to help out for a couple of nights. We can drive mother and Geraldine back to Athens to spare them the bus ride. When we've dropped them off at the airport we can book into a swanky hotel in Athens and have that luxury mini-break you're always hankering after, you'll certainly deserve it after a week of putting up with my mother," I said, delighting Marigold.

"Oh Victor, that would be absolutely wonderful. And you do realise what date it is on Saturday."

"No."

"It's the fourteenth, it's your birthday, it is perfect. We can celebrate your first ever real birthday in style, in Athens. Oh, but what about the cats?"

"I'm sure Barry is more than capable," I replied.

Reaching the top of the track, we turned around to admire the view, resting in the shade of a gnarled old olive tree. White clouds skirted across the blue sky, meeting the distant blue of the sea on the horizon, barely discernible white flecks in the water indicating the sea was choppy. I reflected that our life was good, and with luck it would be nothing but plain sailing ahead in our continuing Greek adventure.

A Note from Victor

All Amazon reviews most welcome.
Please feel free to drop a line if you would like
information on the release date of future vol-
umes in the Bucket series.

vdbucket@gmail.com

Printed in Great Britain
by Amazon

70288637R00174